The Rogue *of* Publishers' Row

The Rogue *of* Publishers' Row

Confessions of a Publisher

by EDWARD UHLAN

A BANNER BOOK

EXPOSITION PRESS • NEW YORK

First Printing, 1956
Second Printing, 1956
Third Printing, 1956
Fourth Printing, 1960
Fifth Printing, 1960
Sixth Printing, 1962
Seventh Printing, 1962
Eighth Printing, 1962
Ninth Printing, 1963
Tenth Printing, 1963
Eleventh Printing, 1964
Twelfth Printing, 1964
Thirteenth Printing, 1965
Fourteenth Printing, 1966
Fifteenth Printing, 1967
Sixteenth Printing, 1968
Seventeenth Printing, 1968
Eighteenth Printing, 1969
Nineteenth Printing, 1970
Twentieth Printing, 1970
Twenty-first Printing, 1970
Twenty-second Printing, 1971
Twenty-third Printing, 1971
Twenty-fourth Printing, 1971
Twenty-fifth Printing, 1972
Twenty-sixth Printing, 1972
Twenty-seventh Printing, 1972
Twenty-eighth Printing, 1972
Twenty-ninth Printing, 1973
Thirtieth Printing, 1973
Thirty-first Printing, 1973
Thirty-second Printing, 1973
Thirty-third Printing, 1973
Thirty-fourth Printing, 1973
Thirty-fifth Printing, 1973
Thirty-sixth Printing, 1974
Thirty-seventh Printing, 1974
Thirty-eighth Printing, 1974
Thirty-ninth Printing, 1974
Fortieth Printing, 1974

ISBN 0-40104-8

LIBRARY OF CONGRESS CATALOG CARD NUMBER: 56-8721

To my children,
ADAM, ABBY and LINDA

Contents

The Rogue *of* Publishers' Row

CHAPTER I

On the Left Hand of God

The book publisher is a lionized and misunderstood curiosity in this civilization of bankers and bathtubs. To most Americans he is a necessary but negligible appendage to the glorious achievements of a Dale Carnegie, a Kathleen Winsor or a Mickey Spillane. To the eccentric fringe of Americans classified as writers, he is sometimes a despotic deity who, by the simple act of publishing an unsung Ozark, can take him from the dungheaps and immerse him in riches and the drool of a thousand literary teacups—or who, by turning a blind eye to obvious talent, can make an author set fire to her home with nine hundred blazing pages of a new (and better) *Gone With the Wind.*

The publisher himself knows that he is a generous and daring financier whose acumen alone keeps Parnassus from crumbling, who is in business for the glory of the sport and who wouldn't desert the game for all the gold in Fort Knox. He is traditionally pictured as dwelling in an ivory tower, in certainly no less favorable a position than on the right hand of God.

Almost all that has been written about publishers and publishing concerns itself with "commercial" (or "trade") publishing. But there is a left hand to publishing too, though the subsidy (or co-operative, or vanity) publisher has rarely ever been written about, except with a tar brush. It seems time to say something about the thousand-odd books and authors published each year in spite of rejection slips that the authors have not accepted as the Word of God.

Almost everyone at one time or another in his life says, "I could write a book." There must be at least a million people who seriously intend to or have tried to. At one time I had an active list of 135,000 people who wrote verse; this gave a little indication of the total number of unrecognized writers in all fields. On any given day in New York, there are some 50,000 manuscripts reposing in the files of the various publishers; and in one year alone, one house lamented, it was offered 10,000 manuscripts.

Since only about 11,000 books are published each year in the United States, it would appear that the odds against having a commercial book-length manuscript published are about a hundred to one. And yet many of the 99-out-of-100 writers have something worth saying, and insist on saying it. Concern for these ninety and nine is my special province, for except for the few who eventually find a place in the publishing program of one of the university presses, to be published at all they must turn to the subsidy house.

It is yet to be determined whether publishing is a business or a profession. Unlike such professions as medicine that have their Oaths of Hippocrates, or law with their bar associations, publishers have no established code or arbiter of ethics. The field being neither fish nor fowl, every publisher has been asked at least once to outline his "philosophy of publishing," and these "philosophies" usually involve both the status of the profession and some concept of public service and responsibility.

My reply, when I am interviewed about my philosophy of publishing, goes something like this: Granted that contemporary subsidy publishing was conceived in sin and dedicated to fraud, we have much important literature of the late-nineteenth and of the twentieth century to prove that it is the practitioners, not the practice, that deserve the criticism. My most important problem is to resist the temptation of larceny that is inherent in any business operation when someone places his faith and trust in you.

To write this book slickly would have been easier than to write it honestly. Sincerity is what you believe and *practice*. But values change with time and growth, even though once you have taken your stand between the covers of a book you are committed to what you have written for so long as it is read. I am therefore aware of the folly I commit by following the footsteps of the many whose books I have seen into the world. This is my book; I conceived it, I lived it, I wrote it and I published it. No one else can be shot; the responsibility appalls me. Still, maybe I summarized my reasons for writing it in a quatrain I wrote in high school paraphrasing the scoffing answer of a promiscuous classmate when I warned her against going out with some boys who talked about her:

> Oh, boys will kiss and boys will tell,
> Which perhaps is just as well,
> For this is but a form of praise,
> And advertising always pays.

Publishing is an endless procession of surprises; when a manuscript is dropped on my desk, out pops the author, often in a guise he wouldn't recognize. I would probably heatedly repudiate the picture of myself that the reader will have formed when finishing the book, yet it will be truer than any self-portrait I could paint.

My kind of publishing is a day-by-day adventure, and the more successful I become, the heavier become the temptations, the worse the risk. Contrary to the belief of some, we will not publish *any* book, no matter how much we are offered. We have rejected as many books as we have published, for reasons that will become apparent in a later chapter. We may growl when ethics tread on my toes, but we heed the warning.

I could write that I became a subsidy publisher out of an altruistic desire to increase the sum total of world knowledge by publishing books that otherwise would never be printed. It wouldn't be true. I went into the subsidy business to make money and am still in it for the same reason. But in order to make money, I had to overcome more than the usual hazards encountered in founding a business. I had to overcome a mass of prejudice caused by mistaken and often fraudulent practices of publishers who had been in the business before me.

I am still fighting prejudice in the only way open to me, by proving it ill-founded so far as my own methods are concerned. I propose to tell in these pages the story of that battle, which is more personal to me than it might have been to another man, because I had to fight my own ignorance and infirmities. I had to rise above considerable physical handicap: I was left crippled by polio in early boyhood. My earliest years were spent in the slums. All this the reader will have to learn about, I suppose, because a book, like a business, is an extension of the individual, and its appeal must be in the reader's interest in the man as well as in his opinions and labors. I doubt if any publisher in New York began as I did; and while some among them have ended in the gutter, I came from where it was our only playground.

Now, climbing from oblivion and not slipping back into it requires a steady gait, and this I found I could acquire only by examining the faults and crimes of my precedessors. I had no source of reference to subsidy publishing other than the lawsuits in which publishers had become involved. If I could find out what sent some men to jail, perhaps I could stay out of it.

There are at least a dozen classic cases of fraudulent publishing, mostly arising out of "come-on" form letters which authors seemed to have found irresistible, and the callous treatment the authors suffered in the form of extortionate costs and shabby and slipshod production. What interested me most was the fact that many books survived their inefficient publication and made money and reputations. It occurred to me that if I could operate a subsidy-publishing business and not be tempted to commit larceny, I would, if I kept at it long enough, build a solid business.

I believed then and believe still that publishing is no different from any other business, in that to be successful you must give value and satisfaction. People would be willing, I thought, to pay for my services providing they knew what they were getting and paying for—and got it. This conclusion has been the cornerstone of my business philosophy and practice, but I am not kidding myself any more than I am kidding you: honesty is the best policy because it pays.

The satisfaction and pride that an author has in his book, especially his first book, is second only to the love a mother feels for her first-born; subsequent children may come and go, but more pain and therefore more pride comes with the first one. It follows that the babies ought not to greet the world in shabby clothing. I get nearly as big a kick out of a well printed and bound book as its author.

There is a certain satisfaction in visiting a home and discovering on the living-room table, wrapped in cellophane and stamped in gold, a poetry anthology containing a poem—*the* poem—the housewife wrote fifteen years before. A page of print and her name on the cover has forever lifted her out of the mass: to her friends and herself she is an author.

From the beginning I published books as well as I knew how—and fortunately I was raised in the bookbinding trade—but it was a long while before my efforts achieved recognition. I can remember the first time a newspaper clipping mentioned Exposition Press favorably. I ought to remember it, for from then dated a whole new set of troubles. I began to be besieged by perverts, crackpots and propagandists. Their money was good; their books were evil. I refused manuscript after manuscript, some with checks attached, because their slime would have coated my business and damaged the reputation I was trying to build up.

One type of book comes to my office with unfailing regularity, that of the homosexual trying to explain why he is what he is and seeking approval as a member of society. It is important that a publisher should be psychologically oriented if he is not to hurt well-meaning authors. He must learn that vice taints him as much as it taints the author—more, perhaps, for while the poor wretch of a writer may be writing under psychopathic compulsion, the publisher is furthering his ends only for one purpose—to make money.

It's hard to know where to draw the line. A woman offered me a manuscript describing how she could murder her husband, the other woman, her inlaws, and get away with it. She wanted six copies. I asked her why and she said she intended to mail a copy to each of her fancied victims. I published the book for her and to date no one has been murdered; it was better, I reasoned, to let her do her killing between the covers of a book rather than those of a bed.

The uncensored story of American publishing won't be

found in the autobiographies of Ludwig Lewisohn, George Macy or Van Wyck Brooks. I have often felt that the desk in my office might be exchanged profitably for an analyst's couch. It is occasionally difficult to discern the difference between the literary and libidinous urges of some female writers who come to see me with their psyches showing, though often they are not aware of it.

A befurred Fifth Avenue matron, a devoted cultist, brought me her religious poetry to publish. As I read her stanzas it struck me that if "he" or "him" was substituted for the word "God," the verses would make some pretty erotic stuff. "Now that you have brought me these," I ventured, "how about the really intimate poems you think are too daring to be shown?"

"How did you know that?" she gasped. I had meant the interpellation as a joke, but on her next visit the poetess had a new sheaf of manuscript under her arm. I had guessed too well.

I have had male authors who have thought they could topple the stars with a spitball. One professor said he could, in ten pages, "disprove" Einstein's Theory of Relativity. A Miami man wrote that his manuscript on the mysteries of the Hebrew alphabet would outsell *Gone With the Wind,* because every Jew would want to buy it—and look how many Jews there are. A French nobleman came in with a pschoanalytical study of Napoleon; the Emperor's belligerency, he announced, had been nothing more than a compensation for the insufficiency of a portion of the anatomy which has always played an eloquent role in a Frenchman's recreations. (Included in his manuscript was a letter allegedly from Josephine in which she said stoically to a friend, "I like the Emperor in spite of his obvious romantic shortcomings.")

An author submitted a formidable array of blueprints and

technical data proving that he could shift the center of gravity so that automobiles, battleships and skyscrapers would find themselves floating on air. The U. S. Government had, he said, offered him fifty million dollars for the invention, and if I would print a million copies of his book he would . . . At this point I interrupted to tell him I would have to charge him a million dollars for the printing. He didn't bat an eyelash, but somehow the deal didn't materialize.

The new writer usually has too much confidence both in his solution to world problems and in the ability of the world as a whole to stand up and take notice of his book the day after publication, and then to buy it eagerly by the tens of thousands. To sober him, I frequently resort to a line from an unkind reviewer who was less than convinced by one of my books: "If he is intent on conveying a message, he should have used Western Union: it's shorter and cheaper."

I have had hopefuls offer to mortgage their homes and sell their cars to pay me for publishing their books. One offered me his 150-acre ranch in New Mexico. Another tried to lure me with a slice of her impending alimony settlement. When she relayed my letter, quoting a price, to her husband, he decided it would be cheaper to stay married.

I have said that my business is with the 99-out-of-100 writers, those who are refused publication by the trade. I will go further. Fully half of the volumes I publish contain valuable source material and information useful in research and education. Of the other half, perhaps a third are theses or theories reflecting a new light on history and human problems. The remainder constitute the reason we are called a "vanity" press; they are valuable only in the pride their authors and their friends feel in a well designed and printed book. Curiously enough, I personally get a good deal of pleasure out of this last category, and I go out of my way to help such authors. It's an odd way to make people happy, but the sum total of their happiness is not to be discounted in the total achievement.

Unlike most trade publishers, we are not obliged to "balance" our catalogue: we do not refuse a cookbook, for instance, because we have two cookbooks already on our list. We publish any and every sort of book except the vicious ones, and here again we have an advantage over the trade publisher: we are not obliged to seek a certain amount of pornography in order to balance our books. We do not have to tell a writer (as one of my acquaintances was told by a trade-book editor), "The boy and girl should go to bed in this chapter." On the other hand, we have no sanctimonious attitude in the matter: if an author thinks his integrity requires a sexual emphasis, that's all right with us, providing it's all right, too, with the Postmaster General.

In other words, we are not in the position of having to dictate to an author what he shall write. Our editors often, almost always, have suggestions for the improvement of manuscripts, but it's the author who is paying for the book, and his is often the last word.

In the last four years we published about eight hundred books, among them novels, biographies, autobiographies, travel books, cookbooks, poetry, how-to-do-it books, religious books, histories, schoolbooks and works of philosophy. No trade publisher could be more catholic in his list because, while our primary interest is the same as his—that is, to sell books—we also cheerfully catalogue books that are not likely to sell at all.

We can do this because we are paid to do it. Just as all publishers do, we push books that show a tendency to sell, but every book we issue is given its chance on the market. No books, except those definitely limited in circulation by their authors, go out without an individual sales job, including review copies, publicity and advertising. This is part of the contract with the author.

All trade publishers, of course, can and do publish books that are subsidized by their authors—some of the most famous best-sellers, as will be seen later, were subsidized originally—and we in our turn occasionally publish books at our own risk either for reasons of prestige or because we think they will make money. In matters of production, exploitation and selling, our methods are identical with those of other publishers. That is, we do the best publishing job possible, and here we have a slight edge over all but the biggest trade publishers because our volume of production allows quality production at the lowest unit cost. In the long run "trade" and "subsidy" publishing are not as mutually exclusive as many suppose.

Only mushrooms could thrive in the little light thrown on many aspects of publishing. The age of the guild, in which trade secrets were handed down from father to son, still thrives, and publishing knowhow is a moth-eaten tapestry of figment and fiction. But every now and then a phase of trade publishing makes news; and when it broke in *Time* magazine in July, 1955, publishers apologized for making money—because it came from subsidized publishing.

Time, in a review headed "The Commercials," reported that Max Miller, author of twenty-four books, had written *Speak to the Earth,* a book on the petroleum industry written on order for DuPont, which paid him about $25,000 for it and also guaranteed the publisher against loss by buying a special edition for oil executives. Other writers in this "industrial" field, it reported, are Bob Considine, who wrote *Man*

Against Fire (Doubleday) about the fire-insurance business, Frank J. Taylor, who wrote *Black Bonanza, Southern Pacific,* and Robert J. Casey (*The Lackawanna Story, Pioneer Railroad*). Giant organizations, from Standard Oil of New Jersey down, are willing to pour money into the pockets of writers and the coffers of trade publishers.

But are trade publishers appreciative? Do they make a public declaration that here is a profitable phase of publishing? They do, but after publishers were interviewed here is how *Time* reported it:

> Almost every publishing house now goes in for commercials that are subsidized by a corporation's pledge to buy from 2,000 to 50,000 copies. Publishers generally are careful, however, not to include more than two or three such titles in their annual lists, lest they get a name for subsidized books. Editors explain that such riskproof deals enable them to take longer chances on other worthy books. Authors like company-commissioned books because the large and steady income helps set them up to write other books.

There is, after all, much to look forward to in publishing, because there are as many reasons for publishing books as for writing them. Pulitzer-prize winner Marquis James has written for money—and glory—classic histories of the Bank of America, Metropolitan Life and the Insurance Company of North America. But it was his ability, not his integrity, that was for sale. Although he had received $100,000 for preparing a life of the founder of W. R. Grace & Company, when company policy clashed with his point of view, he withdrew and the book was never published. Alec Waugh, who was commissioned to write the biography of Sir Thomas Lipton, was not only paid handsomely for the writing but made additional profits, as do many other writers, on royalties.

I believe that every author should have the right to determine whether his book gets published or not, whether financed by himself or by some interested group—perhaps it is this realistic attitude that has made me a controversial figure in publishing. But if big business wants a publishing service, I'll accept their offers. And I'll not pretend that I atone for it by publishing "other worthy books"; on the contrary, a book is worthy of publication or it is not, and no moral judgment will be rendered on the tenuous basis of who is footing the bills.

One thing seems clear to me: if we in the subsidy-publishing business are not gamblers, neither are trade-book publishers. There was a time when every publishing venture was a gamble, a day when publishers—*some* publishers—had a sense of duty that caused them to accept and publish manuscripts which they knew would not sell but which they considered valuable in artistic or educational interest. Such a publisher was Sylvia Beach, whose Shakespeare Book Shop in the Rue de l'Odéon published *Ulysses,* a book which has influenced the literary trends of a century. Miss Beach and James Joyce were rewarded by a fortune neither had expected, but the fact that the banning of *Ulysses* by United States and British censors made the book a world best-seller ought not to detract from the debt the world of literature owes to Miss Beach for publishing it. *Ulysses,* however, was almost the last book so published. Costs of production today forbid gambling. In some respects a publisher's list today resembles that of a bookmaker: he must win enough out of some of his entries to make a profit on the whole. He can't do this if he knowingly accepts a manuscript that has no chance to sell.

Barely twenty years ago, before this last war, a publisher figured to cover his production costs and advance royalties by selling 1,000 copies. Today costs have risen so that a first edition of 10,000 is necessary for the publisher to make a profit. In addition, the trade publisher now (and we also) faces the formidable competition of the paper-backs, which have almost driven the circulating libraries (and with them all cheap romantic fiction) out of business.

These things we shall take up in detail elsewhere, together with my own solution of the publishing problem. There is one other fact that must be dealt with first. However I regret it, the publishing business is no different from most other businesses in that success or failure depends on the aptitude, vision, imagination, courage and persistence of one man or of a group. Moreover, the value of what I have to say depends on what authority I have to say it. I am therefore obliged, though against my inclination, to become personal.

I began in the subsidy-publishing business with fifteen dollars in my pocket and a load of enthusiasm you couldn't put a price on. Last year, in terms of the number of books published, Exposition became the sixth-largest publishing house in the United States. The top house on the list had been in the field for a century or more.

How this came about is the burden of my tale. Let me recline now on a metaphorical couch and "tell all." Not all of it is pretty.

CHAPTER II

Candidates for Oblivion

As a youngster I was a front-running candidate for oblivion. Brought up in Hell's Kitchen, one of Manhattan's toughest slums, at four I was stricken with polio and lay paralyzed for months with only my eyes and mouth alive. When gradually other muscles awoke to usefulness and my body to stabs of pain, my legs were still lifeless; they would not respond to the pricking of needles or to the prodding of my will. They were put into twenty pounds of steel braces, and the first step that I took in them was the real beginning of my education.

From the age of five to my twelfth birthday, between operations, I spent most of my time in pathetically run city convalescent homes, learning to adapt myself physically and psychologically to a minimum level of existence. With other kids who had drawn deuces, I learned the first maxim in *Poor Richard's Almanac*: that one could get things out of people (in our world, chiefly doctors and nurses) for unfathomable reasons.

Only the older children possessed wheel chairs; there weren't enough to go around. And so, in the middle of the night, when the nurse would disappear from her desk, I would crawl from my bed into the nearest wheel chair. It was a thrill to whirl in one of these chariots, almost like rising from the dead. One evening, scooting out on the terrace, I surprised the nurse and an intern playing doctor. They sealed my lips and freed my body; if this was blackmail, I did not know it, but from then on I was the only six-year-old to have a wheel chair all his own.

In convalescent homes I learned also the business of getting something out of someone for a price. With the contents of food packages my mother had sent me, I inveigled a fascinating storyteller among the older boys into spinning yarns for me. A chocolate bar was good for *Jack and the Beanstalk;* a banana would buy *Bluebeard* or *The King of the Golden River,* and a box of crackers *The Ugly Duckling*. My friend, however, was a cold-blooded proposition; as soon as he got his fists on my food he'd quit. I suspect to this day that he gave me crooked weight and that there's more to *Jack and the Beanstalk* than he gave me.

Today the tables are turned. The yarn-spinners now pay me.

We kids in the convalescent homes were gamblers. Not for money, because we had little, but for bottletops, toothpicks, safety pins, or what-have-you, which were six-for-a-penny chips. In a way it was with us as it was with captive Europeans in the last war who made American cigarettes their medium of exchange.

I have many memories to balance those of bitterness. There was the time I cornered the safety-pin market. But I was a sucker for sobs; when one kid told me he was going to run away from the home I liquidated my holdings and lent him my entire capital, fifty cents, only to be told when he came back a few hours later that he had spent my fortune in an ice-cream parlor while waiting for the train.

We were tough and we could smile, but sometimes our hearts were broken. When I was eight my parents sent me to a summer camp for boys with polio. I was bribed to go there with promises that the camp had a wonderful game room, but some bureaucrat beyond the world of crippled boys had snarled up supplies so that when we entered the game room we found it had been fitted up only for girls, with knitting kits, embroidery sets, jacks and dolls. The nurses organized knitting projects, but because the wool supply was limited they had to rip up our work and make us start over again whenever we missed a stitch. I managed to swipe odds and ends of wool and in secret worked on a sweater more colorful than Jacob's coat. When I had completed the two sides I showed them to a nurse; it surprised her into tears.

This incident may seem trivial; in reality it was tremendous. I had learned that an achievement could be woven not only out of dreams but of reality, if the weaver, however handicapped, stuck doggedly to the task. Bit by bit I took heart in little triumphs of strength and will. At first I got from one place to another by crawling; then I moved forward in braces; finally, although doctors had said I could never walk, I took steps without the help of steel.

Even to this day I can't describe exactly what I did that made me walk. It wasn't prayer and it wasn't faith. It may have been a fighting resentment. But I would say that my first real step was taken on the day I purged myself of self-pity and got up one more time than I fell.

Today all over the world there are youngsters struggling to walk unaided. Most of them won't learn to walk in weeks or months, even with modern appliances. Yet notice the face of the next polio victim you come across and you will see that his pain is lost in the exaltation of effort. He doesn't want pity—why should he? He is proud—he has been given an opportunity to win victory over himself. When he succeeds the memory of his pain fades, but the *accomplishment* he can cling to forever.

But before that victory is gained, one lives in a wasteland of helplessness. One particular memory lives like a leitmotif. When I was five, my father took me to the movies and there was a fire. In the stampede that followed my father snatched me up and, calling, "Let this crippled child through!" started for the exit. Not a single person made way for him, he had to push and shove like everybody else, and only his strength made our escape possible. From then on, fear goaded me on to become strong and self-reliant.

One of the vampires a crippled boy must drive a stake through is the zombi of supersensitivity, the fear of curious and pitying eyes, the cruelty of other children. On the day I could walk into a public place without feeling a hundred eyes drilling into me, my affliction became less important than my purpose. I had put polio in its place; there were things my condition prevented me from doing, but the world was full of other things I could do if I learned them.

There's a story my grandfather told that illustrates the attitude I found myself adopting. When the ship in which he was approaching the New World ran into days of tempestuous seas and virtually everybody succumbed to seasickness, Grandfather never missed a meal. When waiters congratulated him, he said he had a system: he had a rocking chair in his cabin and rocked with it and the heaving seas. Gradually, like Grandfather, I learned to rock.

I came to realize that while men were not born equal in terms of physique, health and brains, God had certainly equipped each individual to be equal to his own problems; the secret of survival lay in a man's resourcefulness in turning his liabilities into strength. With a single tool, the ax, the pioneers had civilized a wilderness; the Eskimo, warming himself in snowbanks, fishing through ice, had built his own culture from the same elements that threatened his destruction.

Even a man without legs could make life work for him if he pitted against his disability the power of other muscles and the knowledge in his head.

Nevertheless, it was no easy matter to normalize my life. It was a challenge to be the only Jewish boy in twenty blocks of slums among Dead End kids. I learned to use my fists; I fought for the respect of my cronies, and appealing to their vanity and sportsmanship, I taunted them into abiding by special rules of the game—to fight me from a sitting position or standing in a narrow hallway where I could lean against the wall. Slugging with my back to the wall, trading punch for punch, made me a man among men, and unvanquishable. Soon the toughness of any kid for blocks around was measured by his willingness to fight me under the special rules.

I exulted in my strength, but I learned pity too. This was part of my education in power. When I was twelve, I got into a fight with a boy who had tripped me to the pavement, straddled me, and began to pound me mercilessly. Wild with pain and fury, I hauled off and hit him on his Adam's apple. His face went livid as he fell beside me sobbing for breath, and for a terrible moment my own heart almost stopped. I thought I had killed him. When he revived, we both began to cry, and it was the last time I ever used my fists to win an argument.

In building myself up physically I bent out of shape practically every wrought-iron bar in the tenement staircase. After a while I could rip a telephone book in two and tear a pack of cards in halves. In the neighborhood gym I learned to wrestle, and since I could not topple an opponent from a standing position I would concede him three points and let him begin the match on top of me, a handicap that meant I could not win on points but had to pin his shoulders to the mat. The strength of my arms, coupled with an exhaustive study of every possible armhold, enabled me in one tournament to win in five weight divisions, averaging less than two minutes per match. When I showed Mom the clippings (my athletic activities were conducted in secret), all she could gasp was, "You could've been hurt."

My experiences on the baseball diamond paralleled those in the gym. To be accepted by a physically normal kid on equal terms, I had to outdo him; I made the team because I was the only kid willing to catch a baseball barehanded—an asset because of the scarcity of gloves. I learned to snap a ball from homeplate to second even while my lack of balance had me falling in every direction; when I batted, a substitute ran bases for me.

Although I was unable to use my legs in swimming, I held my own in the water. Once when I was standing near a pool a bather stumbled into the deep end and went under. I was the only other person present. I dived in and literally shoved him into shallower water, and from there jiu-jitsued him through the air to the edge of the pool. I wrenched my back, but he didn't drown.

Today as I look back on these experiences I tell myself that the three most thrilling moments in a man's existence are the first time he makes love, the first time he catches a fish and the occasion on which he saves a human life, all activities usually associated with able-bodied men.

There is still another experience the memory of which steps up my pulse—the first time I piloted my boat out of sight of land. On the bridge of my 36-foot cruiser I have had built a horizontal bar; by gripping this and vaulting six feet or so I can handle the boat from either bridge or deck and be my own skipper.

One of the members of my yacht club once pointed out to me that it was very dangerous for me to take my boat out alone, because I could very easily hurt myself and be incapacitated. My flippant reply was, "There are so many ways of dying—what's one more!" It occurs to me that no matter how ill-equipped or handicapped a person is, he can assume additional risks. After all, the most fabulously well co-ordinated athletes take risks, and calculated ones at that. There is one word of advice that I would give to guardians of people who are handicapped, and that is let them take a calculated risk, because if they are to survive they'll have to do so throughout their lives.

This is a story about books, not about boats; but the sea was one of the challenges I met, and as with Franklin D. Roosevelt, it exhilarated me. I have my private gods. Lord Nelson, blind in one eye and with only one arm but indomitable as he paced the bridge, is one of them. Arthur Kavanaugh, the Irish statesman who was born without arms or legs and yet navigated his sloop around the world, writing descriptions of the sea with a pen attached to a hook on his shoulder, is another. And like Ahab, in the spume and foam of a turbulent life I must hunt the white whale of fate with a harpoon of daring.

As I matured in years and looked about me I perceived an astonishing fact: that my struggles against oblivion were by no means unique or confined to the physically handicapped, that there were numbers of folk who limped through life with invisible scars and welts, who had been paralyzed not by a virus but by a society. I learned especially well that the history of the creative arts, for instance, is filled with stories of artists the world rejected who suffered in the pariah kingdom of the psychically mutilated, with every step toward recognition a milestone of tragedy. Many years later, bent on becoming a publisher myself, I studied the unwitting role some publishers had played in the torture of genius. I learned what had been done to Theodore Dreiser and James Joyce and Herman Melville and Edward Fitzgerald and Daniel Defoe and Arnold Bennett and Upton Sinclair, to note a few on a long and saddening list.

If one doubts whether genius is an affliction, he should review the efforts of Theodore Dreiser to give the world his first masterpiece. The first publisher to reject *Sister Carrie* informed Dreiser that he doubted if any house would accept such a "sordid novel." The second exploded, "The book not merely is vulgar; it hints that the wages of sin might easily be *success!*" When Dreiser submitted *Sister Carrie* to a third house, the girl at the reception desk handed the manuscript back to him saying that the staff did not even care to comment on it. Still another editor advised him to quit writing and to try something "useful."

For the next three years Dreiser lived through a prolonged nightmare. He had spent most of his savings in writing his novel. When his money ran out he applied unsuccessfully for employment with a sugar refinery and a trolley-car company. He stood in line outside factories and shops for piecemeal work. He moved into a furnished room that cost a dollar and a quarter a week; he limited himself at first to two meals a day, then to one, then to a bottle of milk and scraps of bread supplemented by a vegetable he picked up now and then under a stand in a public market.

Breaking down physically, he walked around in a condition of semi-wakefulness, uncertain as to who he actually was. Nights he would awaken with a start, convinced that there was an intruder creeping about his room. He would grab at a phantom hand touching his pillow and withdraw his fingers in a sweat. One evening, after making the usual round of newspaper offices, printing shops and factories for work, he wandered down to the East River to end his life, but he was interrupted by a drunk who danced around him, kicking his legs and singing a ribald old saloon ditty. A canal boatman called out from the shadows, offering him a free ride to Tonawanda, "You look as though you are running away from your wife!" The incongruity of the remark and the jesting of the drunk dissipated Dreiser's black spell of despair. He laughed—for the first time in months. He returned home; and that night he slept soundly.

Today no one remembers the names of the editors who turned down *Sister Carrie*. Dreiser harpooned the white whale and survived.

Martyrdom's long list included James Joyce. He spent five years writing *Ulysses,* during which time his eyes gave out. One evening while walking down the street he had a sudden attack in his right eye. For half an hour he was unable to proceed, and he was carried to a bench. Around the arc lights he saw spinning rainbows. The doctor's verdict: glaucoma. In a hospital a surgeon cut a triangular piece out of the afflicted eyeball. The disease spread to the other eye. At times the agony was so acute that he rolled on the floor in spasms. Yet between operations he continued to work by day as a poorly paid tutor in Zurich and by night to torture his eyes further with *Ulysses.* As he worked on this book and its successor, *Finnegan's Wake,* he underwent nine operations.

When *Ulysses,* later hailed by one critic as "the greatest novel of the twentieth century" and by others compared to the masterpieces of Rabelais, was finished, no publisher could be found. It was, they said, cryptic, corruptive and obscene.

Finally Sylvia Beach, urged by Joyce's friend, Ezra Pound, printed a thousand copies at her own expense, in Paris.

After a while copies reached England and the United States and were promptly banned there—in America by the Postmaster General and in England by the Lord Chamberlain. It became an international sport to get *Ulysses* by the customs: one American had a Paris friend send the book a dozen sheets at a time folded in French newspapers. Others sneaked it in at the bottom of trunks or folded in lingerie. One tourist concealed it between the covers of the Bible. There was Prohibition in the United States, but there were ways you could get liquor off the boat and many a copy of *Ulysses* came ashore in a crate of scotch.

Within a few years of its publication copies of the book that nobody wanted were selling for a hundred dollars apiece. But none of this could buy back Joyce's health or eradicate his years of misery; when he died in Switzerland during World War II he was totally blind.

The agony of rejected genius haunts the sanctum of every publisher who turns down the manuscript of today's unknown. I have known these ghosts, and I have long since realized that frustration has a meaning in three dimensions, not just one.

There was Edwin Arlington Robinson, who printed three hundred copies of his first volume of poetry, paying for it himself, dedicating it "to any man, woman or critic who cuts the edges; I have done the top." There was Walt Whitman, who at thirty-six himself set up, in a friend's printshop, the first quarto edition of *Leaves of Grass*. There was Upton Sinclair, today one of the world's most widely read authors, who subsidized his own books for a quarter of a century because no publisher would touch his social message.

Side by side with the record of tragedy and frustration another theme revealed itself—a theme that fascinated and thrilled me. This was the power of survival displayed by the "unwanted," their stubborn clinging to life. I discovered how *Robinson Crusoe* had been turned down by every publisher in England; how Daniel Defoe persisted in peddling it until an obscure little printer took a gamble on publishing it and parlayed his investment into the biggest profits in publishing history.

I learned how Edward Fitzgerald, when he had finished his translation of the *Rubáiyát of Omar Khayyám,* sent it to a publisher who kept the manuscript an entire year without comment. Finally the exasperated author retrieved the poem and had 250 copies printed at his own expense, giving them to a bookseller. For almost two years they lay unwanted on the shelves. Finally the bookseller reduced the price to a penny and dumped the dusty pamphlets into a bargain box outside his door. One day a browser picked up a copy and leafed through it. He bought up the copies and distributed them to his friends.

This was literally a rescue from oblivion. The *Rubáiyát* became the biggest-selling volume in the history of poetry. Millions of copies have been purchased all over the world; many found their way to the shelves of people who had never read another book. Seventy-five years after the bookseller had dropped the *Rubáiyát* into his bargain box at a penny, his heirs sold first-edition copies for a thousand dollars apiece.

There have been numerous other examples of myopia plaguing Publishers' Row. Even so obviously popular a writer as Zane Grey peddled his first book from one house to another unsuccessfully. "I had no money," he wrote of this ordeal. "When all seemed blackest and my spirit was low, I re-read *Betty Zane* and swore the editors were wrong. I borrowed money to publish my work and I hired a printer. And at last I had a book in my hands—a book I had written! It changed my life. I went to the country to live and write. . . . Every year *Betty Zane,* in spite of its crudities, sells more and more. I never changed a line of it. And in these days of the high cost of living, *Betty* helps nobly to keep the wolf from the door."

That is the literary past I marveled over as a background to my own efforts in publishing. Every time I read a manuscript from a fledgling author, I still cannot pass judgment without recalling that Daniel Defoe, Theodore Dreiser, Edward Fitzgerald, Upton Sinclair, Zane Grey, were once considered unprofitable properties by the shrewdest heads in the business. All of them had to subsidize their way to recognition—had to walk forward on their own two feet without the crutches of other people's money, faith or encouragement. Had they succumbed to self-pity, they would have ended up digging ditches, working as library clerks, or (gruesome thought!) performing as editors passing judgment on other works of genius!

There is an iron continuity in the frustrations faced by the author that reaches into the present. The past is not only history but prophecy. Forty years ago Dreiser and Sinclair were ostracized because they dared to be dangerously individualistic in a business that was even then pointing to the lowest common denominator of group appeal. Today book publishing is looked upon even by editors as basically an operation in product merchandising; and writing to be publishable has to be tailored to pattern and taste like clothes and chewing gum.

But all this I found out later, during my early years in the book business. I had better get along and explain how it all started.

CHAPTER III

Look Who's a Publisher

Determination to overcome physical disability was the main psychological factor in my development as a boy. But determination to survive is not enough: a man must have the incentive of a goal ahead and the knowledge necessary to reach it. As it happened, fate filled an inside straight for me. I became a craftsman in one of the essential trades of the publishing business, bookbinding.

I was twelve years old, an age when most lads in my stratum of society started work as messengers or newsboys. Such work being too active for me, I went to work in my uncle's bookbindery and there laid the foundation of the career I have followed since.

My uncle was a craftsman of the old school, a perfectionist in a trade where quality of workmanship counts for much. I learned early that a good book should not be ignobled by slipshod workmanship. And since the depression found us often without work, I spent my time with other idle printers, engravers and typesetters who abounded in the graphic trades, and pestered them with an endless stream of questions about their trades. They appreciated my inquisitiveness and dubbed me "the Professor of Park Row," which was the publishing center at that time.

I worked by hand and at every machine in the shop, and by the time I was twenty I knew (or thought I knew) as much as my uncle. At any rate, I was a fair craftsman. But I was earning pitifully small wages, and it was no part of my plans for the future to work for others all my life. I could have earned more money on the road as a salesman, but my uncle would not hear of it.

"If I let you drive the car with your condition, Ed, and something happened to you, your mother would never forgive me." The same old obstacle, and it was I who had collected the company car in lieu of an old unpaid bill! As a kid I had been told that I would never be able to drive an automobile any more than I would be able to walk normally; but I had made secret experiments with a bedspring and a piece of bailing wire, with which I had contrived a hand throttle, and I knew I could drive as well as anyone else.

My uncle, however, would not be convinced, so I told him that I would have to quit my job. He promised me fifteen dollars' severance pay—as soon as he could collect on some bills—and with less than five dollars in my pocket I walked out on him at the depth of the depression, in 1935.

There were no jobs anywhere except in the CCC or the WPA, and I was eligible for neither. It was July; the industry was at a standstill. I went up to Westchester, where my family was camping, for my first vacation.

I might have lazed away the weeks at the camp, except that a new incentive came into my life. She was young, blond, provocative, but she had a father with ambitions: having no money himself, he was determined that his daughter should retrieve the family fortunes. It was not a casual affair with either of us, and it was my first. I was twenty-three, and this girl's love had liberated me from the half-man status to which I had thought my disability condemned me. For this reason it was the most important affair of my life. I *had* to find some way to overcome her father's hostility to me. During weekends when he came to the camp, I almost went mad simulating complete detachment from his daughter.

The summer was nearly over when I had my inspiration. I would take the girl's father as a business partner! It was a wonderful idea; I was so relieved at having found a solution that I laughed aloud. When I told my sweetheart, she was happy too. "Oh, Ed, how marvelous!" Then she sobered. "But what's the business?" she asked.

I wasn't deflated. I was still floating on a wave of optimism. "I'll tell you about it when we can be alone," I promised.

An idea that had been only vague until then began to take shape. In high school I had been editor of a literary magazine, and I remembered how students had vied with one another to have me accept their poetry. Some had tried to ruin my amateur standing by offering me bribes to accept their contributions. Later, working with my uncle, I bound books for poets who had paid to have their books printed. People would pay to have their poems printed in little magazines or anthologies, and obliging editors and printers were making money out of it.

I went to my girl's father and told him that I was founding a publishing business and that I wanted him to be my partner. He was overwhelmingly flattered and eager (he was a skip-tracer working part time) to pick up additional change. He would furnish his own typewriter, he said, providing I would supply the capital and find the poets. And, since I had calculatingly stressed the fact that we couldn't afford the rental of an office, he offered his home for an office. From then on, working seven days a week became a labor of love.

The girl was very much impressed. A publisher! And of poetry! Our life at the moment was a poem to her and she was overjoyed.

For three months I hibernated in the New York Public Library. I searched the back numbers of newspapers and magazines for poetry, checking the names of the poets with a telephone directory. There are many more poets in the world than you'd believe, but few of them were in telephone directories available to me. It took me ninety days to put together a list of six hundred names and addresses, and I felt just as the Curies must have felt when after sifting tons of pitchblend they extracted a grain of radium.

I now used my uncle's fifteen dollars to buy six hundred postal cards and letterheads. I worked up a sales letter announcing a poetry contest and offering a twenty-five-dollar Liberty Bond for the best poem submitted. This letter I followed with another in which I offered to print the poem in a new anthology; all the poet had to do was subscribe three dollars for one copy, or five dollars for two copies—and for fifty cents extra per volume he could have his name stamped in gold on the cover.

If anyone had brought up the question of ethics, I would have argued then, as I would argue now, that in such a matter ethics and honesty are synonymous: people were willing to pay me for a specified service, and if I performed that service to their satisfaction the moderate profits I made were certainly ethical—and deserved.

With the mailing of the letters I was in business. I called my enterprise the Adastra Publishing Company and I altered my name to Igor Ulianov, feeling that this would be more to the taste of the recherché clientele I was trying to lure. Since I had no funds for stamps, I requested that return postage accompany each manuscript submitted. When the stamp came in from a poet unattached, I would use it for another mailing. When it came glued on a return envelope,

I had to steam it off. I limited myself to a thirty-five-cent lunch daily and I visited my post-office box twice a week to get the mail—I couldn't afford the carfare for daily visits. Despite this strict budgeting, my funds were rapidly exhausted and I had to think of ways to obtain more capital.

One possibility was to go on relief and sell my food coupons. However, relief was not being given to applicants who lived with their parents. It was necessary for me to establish an independent residence—and my parents had to be kept in ignorance. I had a friend living in Washington, and I wrote myself a series of four letters in his name. In the first three letters my friend, as if in answer to my complaints, analyzed my conflict with my parents in painstaking psychological detail. In the fourth letter, he discussed the "visit" he had paid me since his first three letters, to observe at first hand my situation; and he advised me that since matters had deteriorated to a terrible level, I should leave home and set up independent residence. I showed these letters to the interviewer to establish the motive for leaving my parents' home. "How understandingly your friend writes about your domestic problem!" she declared. She couldn't have been less than a Ph.D. in psychology. Needless to say, I never told my unsuspecting friend in Washington about this compliment on my ghostwriting ability. Nor are my parents, to this day, aware of the problems I had with them. I was placed on relief and sold my coupons, which brought in about three dollars a week.

One day three weeks after my initial mailing, my first business turned up. The wife of an Oregon doctor sent a check for five dollars for the publication of her poem and two copies of the book. Since I had no money to open a checking account, cashing the five dollars presented a problem. I recalled that a certain Mendel who owned a neighborhood poolroom cashed checks for anybody who made bets or patronized his tables. I had never held a cue in my life. I went down to Mendel's and played a game with one of the neighborhood pool sharks, at my expense. Then I asked Mendel to cash my check.

"Who's it from?" he asked suspiciously.

"The wife of a doctor."

"O.K. Doctors I trust."

Then he noted that it had been drawn on an Oregon bank.

"This will take at least ten days to clear. I can't do it."

I looked him in the eye and sneered, "So you're Mendel, the big book, and you're worried about waiting ten days for five lousy bucks!"

Flattery won the day and he cashed the check.

This was the beginning of my dealings with Mendel. At first the money trickled in, sending me down to Mendel's twice a week for pool, but as the flow stepped up, I became an expert billiardist.

When I had got together enough poems and orders to print a 128-page book, I was faced with the job of editing the book for the press. I had no formal knowledge of poetry, let alone experience in editing. But these were minor obstacles. I again took up quarters in the New York Public Library—this time for three days—and I went through every book on poetry technique I could lay my hands on. When I had learned what a poem was supposed to be, I saturated myself with information on how to edit it by verse and stanza.

As soon as my anthology, *Diadem of the Muse,* was mailed to my subscribers, I got busy on a second book for new and repeat business. This time I asked each prospect to refer friends to me. But the intervening weeks saw my capital dwindling fast. I kept my assets fluid by indulging in the nightly nickel poker games at the corner drugstore. Although I knew that the proprietor of the store cheated, I once more went to the library and learned how to mark a deck well enough to overcome his clumsy double-dealing and to win about ten dollars a week until the checks came in again.

A rift with my partner was gradual but inevitable. When I discovered that he was secretly copying our list of poets for his own exploitation, I decided that the break must come. I hired desk space at two dollars per month at an impressive Fifth Avenue address and started another company. At one time I ran six different poetry enterprises out of one building, each under a different editorial pseudonym.

Shortly after I broke with my partner, I received a phone call from a Canadian who said he wanted to sell a list of song lyricists he had built up over years of "song shark" publishing. He was a professor of music at one of the Toronto colleges and he had gone into the music-publishing business on the side. The verses he received from his lyricists he handed over to the pupils in his music classes to set melodies to, and he charged the writers money for turning their poetry into songs, and the songs into "hits."

This versatile midwife for the muse had been prospering in his business until he made a fatal misstep. He began promising his poets juicy profits from the sale of their songs. It is amazing how poets who rail against the "poisonous materialism" of the world will suddenly kick their heels like schoolboys at the prospect of becoming contaminated with money—plenty of it. A prolonged diet of immortality alone can leave one hungry. Because the only profits in the venture went into the professor's pocket, the Canadian Government issued a fraud order against him and put him out of business. Since he was also an aspiring poet, he was on my mailing list.

He had a list of 75,000 music-mad versifiers for sale. I snapped at the opportunity. An extensive list like this, much larger than any I believe existed, was exactly what I needed to give my business a needed impetus—providing the professor was on the level with his names and addresses.

"How much do you want for the list?"

"Six hundred dollars."

It was agreed that I would mail him a hundred dollars to have the list forwarded to me and that I would pay the balance upon receipt. But, with visions of the law panting at his heels, I could not contain my anxiety. I took the night train for Toronto and arrived the following morning. I walked into the professor's home.

"Hello, I thought I'd come to Toronto for some fun at the same time. Where is the list?"

The professor, a white-haired, lantern-jawed individual with sardonic eyes, said it was at the other side of town. Within minutes we were in a cab and headed north. We drew up to an isolated, run-down building that bore the modest sign "Nursing Home." Before I could follow the professor to the door, an elaborately dressed, aged Amazon had opened the door and grimaced cheerfully. "The girls have missed you." But the professor was bent on business, and took me directly to a rear room and hauled a suitcase from underneath the bed. Amid the cheap perfume that even the open window could not dispel, he laid the bare frame of his business, reams of neatly typed names, on the bed between us.

I counted out the money in twenty-dollar bills; he threw in the suitcase for good measure, and I made my way back to the cab alone. The professor stayed on to enjoy his money.

Back in New York I decided to run a complete mailing at once to find out whether I had purchased a dud. The mailing was large and exhausted my bank account (by this time I had one). But I need not have worried. Returning from a weekend holiday two weeks later, I found my office girl awed: she had been opening my mail and my desk was covered a foot deep with manuscripts panting for publication. As a result of this mailing I increased my office space and my staff from two to twenty-four, and I was "big business."

In 1936 I decided to give my organization its present name—Exposition Press. In doing so I ran into unexpected difficulty. New York was soon to have its World's Fair, and this gave me the idea for the name. I went down to City Hall and paid the $3.50 required by law for a certificate of title. The clerk had just placed the certificate in my hand when another official rushed over to him and said, "Nobody can take out a business certificate using the name World's Fair or Exposition." The clerk wanted me to return the certificate.

"I paid three fifty for this; it's mine." I walked off.

A month later I received a letter from Grover Whalen, our "Celebrity Greeter" and at that time director of the World's Fair and a member of a very impressive law firm. He informed me that I could not use the name Exposition Press unless I paid for the rights. I replied, pointing out that the term *exposition* not only applied to a fair but to a category of writing, that world's fairs had not been invented by New York City, that I was not operating on the fair grounds and had no intention of implying to anybody that I was connected with the fair.

I thought I had presented my case convincingly; but I received another strong letter from Whalen stating that my arguments were not well taken and that unless I paid for the name I would be in for serious trouble. I replied that the prospect of slugging it out with him and his financially wealthy associates did not frighten me, and that my resources—outside of money—were unlimited, since this was very much a matter of principle with me. With regard to my financial assets, I enclosed a photostatic copy of my bank statement indicating that I had a balance of only three hundred dollars. I did not hear from Whalen again.

My years in the anthology business were rich in the study of human eccentricities. When one goes fishing for poets, one comes up with some extraordinary catches. I was astonished to discover how many uneducated aspirants to the arts had music in their souls. Some of this music, to be sure, sounded like the death rattle of an alley cat being skinned alive, but still it was music of a sort.

One of my contributors, who called herself Queen of the Hoboes, recited her verses in the street for pennies and wrote of God and love while hitching a ride on freights. Another misty-eyed Leader, who styled himself Him That Heareth, jotted down verses that were "prophecies" allegedly spoken into his ear by Jehovah, who favored him above all men living. Him That Heareth stirred up quite a sensation among his disciples and he was actually boomed for the presidency of the United States. This modern Hosea wrote me that he had developed twenty-four basic mathematical formulas according to which all human problems—love, marriage, war, earning a livelihood—could be scientifically solved.

Another of my versifiers I dubbed the Mad Mechanic. He wrote his poetry in a mental institution. Each time he needed money to pay for inclusion of a poem in an anthology (by this time I was selling eager bards space by the page), he used a set of keys made out of horseshoe nails and let himself out of the asylum to take a job. When he had earned enough to send me a money order, he gave up working and returned to the institution. This happened three times in a year, for he wrote a good deal, dedicating his poems to Helen of Troy, Cleopatra, Clara Bow and other girl friends who were in the asylum with him.

I had one poetess who spent ten years rewriting the Bible in rhymed verse. Another client would call me up long distance to read his latest poems so they could be accepted for publication immediately. Sometimes whole families would be bitten by the urge to create; in one anthology I had selections by grandmother, mother and daughters. In another I published the verse of a butcher, a baker, an Indian chieftain and an electrician, all from the same Western town.

No sooner had it become bruited about that I was publishing poets than I was pestered by the song sharks operating on the fringes of Tin Pan Alley. These bunco men preyed on poets, offering to wrap their lyrics in deathless melody for a mere sixty-five dollars or so. When they found a sucker they would hire an assembly-line tunesmith for three dollars and, stealing a bar here and a bar there (anything under four bars could be legally lifted from copyright music), he would slap together a jerry-built melody almost in the time it takes to sneeze. I refused to divulge my list to these sharks and protected my poets as best I could from their forays.

Although the general run of verse I printed was indifferent, I published, of course, first-rate poetry whenever I could get my hands on it. Some of the leading poets of today were published originally in anthologies, for example, Witter Bynner and Laura Benét, Edna St. Vincent Millay. Unfortunately, the real poets were generally poorer than the amateurs, perhaps because they were real.

In charging my poets for publication, I echoed the statements of the general trade publishers: Poetry rarely pays its way. The public reacts to it as though it were some form of bacteria (and I've noticed that it *is* catching, at that). My guess is that this antipathy to poetry is derived from our schooldays. Exposure to verse is a traumatic experience for many a youngster who for punishment had to memorize twenty lines of *The Ancient Mariner* or Homer's *Odyssey,* and no child is given a hint that these bewhiskered poets staring at him from his textbook ever threw a baseball, went to a dance or played hooky from school. To a kid, poets aren't human.

I doubt if present-day poets have a better chance, especially as their stuff is getting less and less easy to memorize, even if they don't wear whiskers. (T. S. Eliot looks like a credit manager; Robinson Jeffers like a cherub, and Louis Untermeyer has been likened to a throat specialist; the only real poets I have known who have looked and acted *like* poets have been Maxwell Bodenheim and Dylan Thomas.)

There is considerable shaking of heads over the lack of a public for poetry, generally attributed to a mass lack of sensitivity. I am convinced, from my own experience, that Americans actually love poetry, providing it is called by another name. "Four score and seven years ago . . ." Isn't that poetry? Our folkways are saturated with poetry. So for that matter are the air waves, if you like singing commercials. And what about the thousands who try to write it? Almost every man and woman has been a poet for some moments of his life. Especially if there's a war; there's a peculiar exaltation in combat that spreads poetry like a rash. When in World War I the AEF was canvassed for poems there were more than seventeen thousand entrants.

Even today, as this book is going to press, about five hundred radio stations are broadcasting poetry programs almost exclusively from Exposition books of popular verse. Of course this took a bit of doing to get started, but, given sufficient co-operation and understanding—and thousands of free books—verse can become a public service . . . even without sponsors.

I am hardly to be considered an expert on poetry (if I were I might have shot myself long ago), but it seems to me that much modern verse falls flat because it lacks virility. Shakespeare wrote lustily, colloquially and at times pornographically, and huge audiences read and declaim him today. And where are the magnificently purple oaths of Chaucer, Donne, Browning, where their wondrous invective? When the prophet interpreted Jehovah as saying, "In the sweat of thy face shalt thou earn thy bread," a multitude thrilled. When the modern poet e. e. cummings writes, "ygurdygur glingth umpssomet hings (whi,le sp,arrow,s wina)," people don't know whether it's poetry or doublecrostics.

Once upon a time poetry was a medium for expressing belly emotions, not cerebral dialectics. What poet today lets off steam as Browning did when, coming across Edward Fitzgerald's posthumously published letter expressing relief at the death of Elizabeth Barrett Browning because now she would "pen no more dull sonnets," he sat down and wrote:

> And were yourself alive, good Fitz,
> How to return your thanks would tax my wits;
> Kicking you seems the common lot of curs—
> While more appropriate greeting lends you grace;
> Surely to spit there glorifies your face—
> Spitting—from lips once sanctified by Hers.

If only Edwin Arlington Robinson, during his lifetime, had been able to get up a good fight with, say, Stephen Vincent Benét over an insult to a woman's reputation, God knows how many thousands of red-blooded Americans would have been attracted to ringside seats! But no modern poet is ever quoted seriously about vital issues. His poetry is disembodied, eviscerated. Looking in it for a meaning related to daily experience is as futile as stringing pearls on cooked spaghetti.

Modern poets are caught in the toils of a dismal cycle. Although publishers rarely expect to make money on them, they will occasionally hang on to a gifted bard, sweating through one unprofitable volume after another in the hope that the author can ultimately be persuaded to write a textbook on poetry or English literature which can be made compulsory reading by boards of education and result in the sale of a million copies. If the poet succumbs to the bait and tailors a textbook to the demands of the educators, he becomes a partner in the conspiracy to turn a new generation of young Americans into lifelong poetry haters.

Although being a poet is not beer and skittles financially, it has its compensations. While there has been virtually no audience for poetry, there has been one for some of the poets. They have been wined and dined and invited to one university after another to give readings before gatherings of the literati. Not one person in twenty at these gatherings bothers to read a published line of the poet, but everybody goes into raptures over the way he rolls his eyes, flashes his bicuspids and declaims his verse. This peripatetic bard is the modern version of the medieval troubadour, and he sings his heart out for food and bed. Frequently his bed is shared by his hostess, so that it cannot be said that his talents were spent on barren ground.

This lionization of the penurious poet has at times been carried to ridiculous extremes. When a portrait painter is invited to a dinner, he is not expected to paint a portrait of the hostess right after the dessert; nor is the sculptor expected to do a bas-relief after downing his brandy. But whenever a poet appears as a guest, hardly has he washed down his last morsel of petits-fours with a stinger, when, as a matter of routine, he is called upon to deliver his latest ode to creation on his not too steady feet.

But to return to our muttons, as the French say, poets and poetry, whether in inverted commas or not, were now my business. And they were good business, too.

During the height of my poetry-anthology days, I became friendly with Henry Harrison, a poet, critic and editor turned publisher who had preceded me in the poetry-publishing field. In 1944, after eighteen years of publishing, he decided to sell his business, which was taking too much time from a new interest that had replaced his interest in Pegasus—those wingless horses running at various race tracks. He asked me to make him an offer. I did, but another publisher offered him three times as much—but with the condition that he needed "time" (a month) to ascertain his exact draft status. The horses were running at Tropical Park in Florida, and Harrison was champing at the bit; so with only twenty minutes for me to take over his business and check his bookkeeping, warehouse stock and other assets he handed me twelve typewritten sheets itemizing the inventory and other matters, grabbed his hat and flew off to catch the next train.

When I investigated what I had bought, I decided that Henry was even more unconventional than I had thought. Sometimes he had carbon copies of correspondence, sometimes not. What bookstore debts he couldn't collect he ignored —and something may be said for that. Despite the haphazard transaction, I recouped every penny of my investment almost immediately by selling as waste paper unsalable, unbound books of verse from the warehouse.

Several months later, when Harrison came back to town, I made him designer and production man. When his two-hour lunches, spent typing out bets and taking them uptown to his bookie, interfered with production schedules, I offered to book his bets. All I knew about horses I had learned from reading *Black Beauty*. The racing form is no match for the law of permutations, and he lost that first day, and every day that week. Each morning for several weeks he handed me a list of his track selections; at the end of every week he adjusted his wages and his losses—sometimes with nothing left over. I never checked his computations; I didn't have to, since I had stayed ahead for almost two years. Then a bookie took over the barber shop in the building, and Henry began getting haircuts on the house while paying to be trimmed.

Harrison was the last of the one-man publishers. He had been among the first to publish and encourage Karl Shapiro, Peter Viereck, Walter Benton and other leading poets. Henry himself wrote a great deal, but unevenly. His first volume contained, said the reviewer for the Salt Lake City *Tribune*, some of the worst stuff imaginable. When I bought his business, his first stipulation was that I agree to destroy every copy of this first book that was in the warehouse. Six years after this book's publication, Harrison had published a second volume, which the same reviewer called a "literary masterpiece deserving the Pulitzer prize for poetry."

Henry is at present poetry manager of my firm and handles 500 radio and TV poetry programs in addition to other incredible tasks. He is an excellent book designer, a master craftsman in an age of assembly-line production. Once he prepared for me on a single typewritten sheet a list of typographic instructions that proved to be the classic summary of rules for designing books of poetry. A number of the top designers in the field still emulate him.

Henry Harrison and his quixotic breed may have glimpsed giants where others saw only windmills, but the poets of today and the little magazines of literature owe much to the pioneer publishers who perpetuated their dreams in print between covers.

Shortly after Henry left me for the first time I decided to branch out into the field of general publishing. I felt that the techniques of dealing with poets were not different from those necessary to handle other writers. There was a subtle difference, however. Poets merely wanted to be published; few had any idea that their *métier* would make them rich. But novelists, dramatists and writers of nonfiction books almost without exception expected to make their fortunes.

I had to be tactful in this matter. He is unwise who culpably destroys hope; besides, these authors have an outside chance of seeing their dreams come true. As I have said already, dozens of books originally subsidized by their authors have made sizable fortunes. But all I promised was the rainbow and denied the existence of the pot of gold.

If I would not deliberately discourage a writer, I would explain the odds and I would point out, which is true, that a first book, even if a failure financially, is an asset when considered as experience. One must buy experience in every trade.

I felt I could satisfy the needs of the novelist unable to find an outlet for his product in the general trade market. There might be many reasons for this, not necessarily having to do with the quality of the novel itself. He might have had a poor agent, or none at all. He might have been refused by a few publishers because they were overloaded with fiction or because his book did not fit in with their lists. He might have been discouraged after one or two refusals, or the book might need a more complete editing than the trade publishers would consider.

There were many books begging to be published for reasons other than dollars and cents. College professors, for example, needed books published to add to their degrees and academic standing, and these were often books on abstruse subjects which appealed to no established market. Then there were the enthusiasts of this hobby or that, burning to reveal their opinions and experiences.

So my asylum for homeless poets was enlarged to accommodate other writers with no publishing roof over their heads. This new departure involved drastic changes in my organization. I had to establish myself as a subsidy publisher who actually took his responsibilities seriously, for only so could I make a solid reputation. It was necessary to play fair with author *and* his public *and* the booksellers.

This, of course, sounds elementary. But it was far removed from the practices of subsidy publishers. Subsidy publishing was more often than not larcenous and fraudulent. Its general unsavoriness was manifest in its very operation. Many subsidy houses were fly-by-night ventures, run from desks rented for as little as two dollars per month—the sum I myself had paid years before when I began to issue poetry anthologies. But there is a vast difference between publishing an occasional anthology and publishing a list of books.

I had the premises and the organization now to give service. I was becoming favorably known to printers and binders, who charged other subsidy publishers the highest possible prices to cover their credit risks, using low-grade labor and seconds in paper and cloth. Until I began business with a whole new set of stipulations born of actual technical knowledge, very few subsidy books came up to trade specifications. Their covers would warp; their sheets would be folded against the grain; typographical errors would be numerous; editing and proofreading would have been ignored and copy set "as is."

I have a vivid memory of an experience when I had first entered the anthology field. I had gone to a rival publisher to purchase the names and addresses of authors who had just appeared in one of his anthologies, and so shabbily had he treated his authors that he knew none of them would publish with him again. Consequently I got the list for a song.

When I walked into his office he was busy wrapping up books in one sheet of wrapping paper and tying them with a piece of string. I assumed that this was ignorance and started to tell him how to ship them, but he cut me short saying, "This is how I ship 'em." I said that wrapped like that the books would be ruined in the mail. He replied that he shipped them express, collect.

To have shipped the books by mail would have cost the publisher twelve cents; when they were sent collect by railway express the author would have to pay a dollar. This was an example of the attitude of such publishers toward the authors, and it was such practices combined with the shoddy quality they gave which made subsidy publishers rightly despised by the publishing fraternity.

One of the more notorious cases I had come across in my study of the business was that of Carlo Flumiani, a subsidy publisher sentenced to eighteen months in prison for fraud. A petty racketeer who had previously milked the public of funds for a quack mental-healing society, Flumiani had turned his talents to publishing, founding several publishing houses and a literary agency which worked together in a diabolical synchronization.

The procedure was as follows: advertising as the Revel Literary Agency, Flumiani solicited manuscripts from authors, charging them fees for revising and marketing them. He would shelve a manuscript for thirty days, and then, in the guise of his publishing houses—the Prometheus, Pegasus, Psychology, Minerva Presses—he would nibble for the manuscript. After each of these houses rejected it in turn and the author was thrown into a nervous fit, a fifth house, Fortuny, Inc., rushed into the picture announcing that it was ready to publish the manuscript if the author agreed "to pay part of the manufacturing costs." The president of Fortuny was listed as a Mr. C. M. Ferra (an alias for Carlo Flumiani).

Flumiani's editor-in-chief was an eighteen-year-old high school girl who received $13.60 a week. She read from fifteen to twenty-five manuscripts a day and made a publication offer for anything that was legible. During the last eighteen months in business, Flumiani published 117 books; his earnings were $92,791; the total in royalties received by his authors was $77.84. Ironically, one of the books Flumiani published was entitled *How to Make Money as an Author*. During this period his staff expanded from six to forty employees, all high school girls working for a pittance.

In sentencing Flumiani, Judge Simon Rifkind pointed out that he had not been found guilty for being a subsidy publisher but for making false promises and for giving authors a dishonest return for their money. One of Flumiani's advertising slogans was, "A Fortune to Gain in Each Fortuny Book." A stock expression used in letters to solicit authors told how the firm had received "encouraging reports considering sales possibilities" of a manuscript. He told one author that he had sent out five hundred review copies of her book when, as a matter of fact, only 150 copies had been printed. A Dominican nun testified that she had paid $1,675 to have a juvenile book published. Flumiani spent $225 to have a thousand copies of the book printed and bound. The Dominican Sisters sold four hundred copies, but received no royalties.

One author who submitted a manuscript to Pegasus House was given the stock pronouncement that his book was "an original work of exquisite quality." When the author balked at the high price demanded for publication, Pegasus suggested that he get a reliable literary agency to place the work elsewhere. It recommended the Revel Agency. Revel shelved the manuscript for sixty days and then announced that it had found a publisher—none other than Fortuny, Inc. Fortuny quoted the same high price as Pegasus; and, to put further pressure on the author, Revel sent him notice that the manuscript had been previously rejected by Prometheus, Psychology and Minerva Presses. But the author refused to be budged. His testimony at the trial was especially damaging.

One of the fake companies Flumiani set up on paper was the Associated Publishers of North America. Whenever an author became suspicious of Flumiani, this "company" would send him a letter endorsing the Flumiani firms as reliable publishing houses. Whenever an author was slow in his payments, a formidable dunning letter came from the Associated Publishers applying decisive pressure.

There are always rotten apples that spoil a barrel. Racketeers will frequently muscle into legitimate operations and turn them into a mockery, bringing the wolves down upon reputable businessmen in the field. As a result of the Flumiani case, publishing as a whole received a nasty, unwarranted stigma.

Despite this, I remained optimistic. I was convinced that

subsidy publishing could be honestly conducted and could fill a genuine need, provided the publisher could not be tempted to indulge in Flumiani's practices.

Nevertheless, immediate conditions were not encouraging. Printers, binders and typesetters treated subsidy publishers with the contempt they deserved. They scheduled these jobs at their own convenience, usually when all the other business had been taken care of.

To launch one of my books I arranged for the author to appear at an autograph party in his home town. However, the binder phoned me at the last moment that he would be four days late with the book. The books had to be cased in and jacketed. All preparations had been made for the party; the invitations had been sent out, and now I was faced with the prospect of having no books to furnish the bookstore.

I rushed down to the bindery, worked on the books myself (overcoat and all) during the weekend (it was December and a boiler breakdown had left the building without heat), piled them into my car and drove to the bookstore—eleven hours through a snowstorm.

The author, whom I had never actually met, was raging up and down the sidewalk; the bookstore was already filling with friends anxious to buy books with his autograph. The sight of me carrying the books into the store was a tremendous relief to him, but his anxiety had been such that he had to let off steam. "You tell that publisher what I think of him, keeping us waiting like this," he yelled.

I said I would personally give the publisher hell. And to this day, he still thinks I was driving the boss's car!

This experience convinced me that I must stop dealing with one-man printers and bedroom binderies if I was to establish a reputable business. I must make certain that my books came out on schedule and in a professional manner. Of course this meant dealing with union shops, whose costs were 10 to 25 per cent higher than the houses with whom I had been doing business. Once I had made the transition, I discovered that it did not cost me or the author any more in the end. I was frequently able to send books to press on second proofs. Deliveries were made promptly and sales were effected sooner. I no longer had to worry about whether the binder had billed me for books that were theoretically bound but actually not finished. I am convinced that a subsidy publisher, to be worth his salt, must serve as an adjunct to trade publishing and that he can do this only by following the practices that make regular publishers the "bright boys" of the packaging industry.

As I look back upon early practices in the subsidy field, I realize that not all was black or even gray. While many of the boys in the game were out-and-out cynics, there were well-intentioned and even genuinely noble figures who were tragically ensnared by their own weaknesses. On one occasion I received news that the head of Decker Press, a subsidy house in Prairie City, Illinois, had been murdered by his partner, who then committed suicide. He had left his business in utter disorder. In some cases, books that had been contracted for were in type, or in printed sheets. There being nobody on the scene capable of stepping in and pushing the work to completion, I decided to buy the publisher's stock and take over his writers. I phoned the attorney for the estate asking permission to examine the inventory. He told me I could rummage through the stock and salvage what I could if I paid five hundred dollars to the estate.

Prairie City had a population of two hundred and sixty-five and one flush toilet, and is stuck in the middle of the

Illinois prairie. The publishing house was a dilapidated one-story building that was also used as a bus depot. In this building the publisher had his printing press, bindery, warehouse and editorial offices.

I found the files in complete confusion. No efficient publishing help had been willing to come out to the little community. I knew that this firm had printed, among other things, the first volume of poetry published by Edgar Lee Masters. I searched for it, realizing that if I could add it to my library the value alone would be worth my trip and the "service charges," but I was unable to find a single copy.

This publisher had acquired the reputation among authors for being a cheat. I myself had heard rumors of his sharp dealing, but in going through his personal correspondence I developed an entirely different picture of him. I found that for years he had drawn only fifteen dollars a week in salary; that at his death he was on the verge of bankruptcy. I was shocked to learn an additional fact: a week before his death he had borrowed money to buy one good suit and had come to New York to ask me for a job. I had been out of town and did not get to see him. This trip had been his final effort to get on his feet.

I visited his living quarters—one shabby room in a corner of the shop. Along one wall were shelves lined with classical records. The beanery next door complained to me that he had been a terrible annoyance to them; he had played his records far into the night, sometimes until the dawn. Beethoven, Mozart, Schubert had been his means of forgetting things . . . and it took the play away from the juke box.

Poring over the haphazard files, I discovered that the unfortunate man had entered the subsidy business when, as a young man, he had written a 320-page poem which he couldn't afford to have published. He approached the Decker Press and offered to pay for publication by working without salary.

He joined the staff, toiled day and night and finally his child was published. Then the owner of the business, a woman, suggested that he might take over its management for a share in the profits. An impractical man, he struggled with the firm through a long series of reverses and when it went under, the lady owner rewarded him for his fidelity by shooting him through the head. Jacob's seven-year labor for the hand of Rachel was no more poignant than this poet's labors for the favor of the muse.

The field I was entering was strewn with the wreckage of good intentions and lofty dreams. I was aware that to survive I would have to avoid the mistakes of my predecessors and conduct my publishing with common sense and have faith that my work would be recognized. Common sense meant fair dealing. In publishing you cannot translate the words any other way.

In the years that followed I made the formula work. Vanity publishing has become co-operative publishing, and some of the nation's most substantial businessmen have become my partners in the publishing of their books. If Mr. Grover Whalen, quondam czar of the World's Fair, ever submits a manuscript to me, I shall gladly offer him my imprint of respectability at a fairer price than he (to my way of thinking) wanted for his.

CHAPTER IV

The Star Wagon

The prison walls that polio had built were crumbling.

When I first broke from my bonds I thought of freedom in terms of money, the nickel that would carry me around the city in a subway train, the price of a specially adapted bicycle to give me wings over the highway, the huge sum that would purchase, if I could ever afford one, an automobile in which to span the continent. For me, money meant movement and a new world of experience.

I was to find there were other freedoms, freedom of the mind from drudgery, freedom of the intellect from superstitions and shibboleths.

But all other freedoms in our civilization are dependent on the first, which is often obtained by the possession of money. Only security can free you for constructive work. Worry over material things throttles the mind. An artist driven by a compulsion to create might paint a masterpiece in a garret, but he still needs money for the pint of *pinard,* the patching of his shoes and an occasional sausage. *Trilby* and *La Bohème* make pretty reading and listening, but I am skeptical of poverty as an incentive to genius, unless it can be overcome. It was not poverty that made Dreiser write *Sister Carrie;* it was the ungovernable instinct in him to create.

While I worked for my uncle I rarely was paid more than two or three dollars a week, for ten hours' work a day. This was "pocket money," because I lived at home. There was an almost unbearable resentment in me against men with a great deal of money, but the resentment took the form of an equally unbearable determination to make enough for myself. This, of course, is no uncommon phenomenon: America is built by it.

But to accumulate money I had to work twice as hard as normal men do, and I had to think my way around "my handicaps," for the men who wanted what I did were willing to work as hard as I did to get it, and had no special problems.

Business did not come to me, I had to go out and get it. One of the first things I did was to educate myself as a public speaker. To put myself on exhibition on a public platform was in itself a difficult decision. But I found that if I had anything real to say the audience was sympathetic; they realized that the real "me" was not my body but what was inside my head.

The first invitation I received was to address an association of American humorists, a group consisting of gag writers and comedians and just about the most cynical audience a fledgling speaker was ever called upon to face. I had been asked to share the platform with Joey Adams, a top-flight professional comedian, and was scheduled to discuss humorous writing from the viewpoint of the book publisher.

As my lecture date approached, the prospect of competing with Joey Adams for the attention of the audience kept me tossing at night. I realized that if Adams ran out of words he could go into one of his bread-and-butter comic routines and "bring down" the house. In contrast to Adams' showmanship, I was certain that my amateurism would make me "speechless" by comparison. I had been told to prepare a ten-minute talk; but when I arrived at the hall, I was horrified to learn that Adams had been delayed and I would have to hold the audience for three-quarters of an hour or longer.

I went before those comedians, feeling like Daniel about to be thrown to the lions. But when I plunged into a discussion of publishing, I really warmed up to my theme. I held the attention of the audience for an hour. For in the audience were "bitter poets," two of whom had appeared in my anthologies. I even kept Adams waiting a few minutes before I got through.

That experience was enough to establish my confidence as a speaker. Since then I have lectured from coast to coast and I have developed many interesting contacts. I recall one Hollywood party I attended at which I was introduced to a well-known movie comedian. We discussed among other things the difficulty an actor has in finding real financial security in Hollywood, where a star can be pitched overnight from the throne into a gutter by the failure of a picture at the box office. This comedian told me that he had invested his money in profitable real estate and that his blood pressure had long since ceased to fluctuate with the returns of the box office. "I'll tell you what *real* security is, Ed. I can ride along Sunset Boulevard and urinate out the door of my Cadillac, and every second building I wet is *mine!*"

In evaluating my life, I was aware that for years I was an outsider looking in at the goodies of life. It was to savor their sweetness that I risked steps to cross the threshold.

When I was a teen-ager, my mother in her well-meaning fashion warned me that because of my physical condition I would have to be content with a humble role all my life and that the only girls that would care for me would be unattractive and poor and therefore appreciative of the little I had to give her.

My mother was mistaken. I have found that there are

personality elements between men and women which transcend physical attractiveness. With the liberation of the spirit which came when I had proved my ability to hold my own with men came a lessening of the shyness which had kept me from legitimate masculine desires. Just as I had found I could command respect from men, so now I learned that love recognizes no barriers. It was because I was anxious to sustain the increasing respect of a beautiful and talented woman that I ventured from anthology publication into general book publishing.

I began with high ambitions: I would publish fifty books a year. Long before the year was up, it was plain that I would have to publish twice as many. My staff grew and continued to grow. My predecessors in the subsidy-publishing field almost always worked alone, because to employ people was to invite competition. When I made the decision to hire an intelligent staff, I felt that I was inviting competition. How right I was, when I can say that at least six of my competitors are people who have previously worked with or for me.

I decided that I would have to do everything that a trade publisher did—do it faster and do it cheaper, since I had to publish on a limited budget. I therefore was one of the first publishers to make a yearly contract with a book designer—Stefan Salter—to design all of my books. I scouted around for talent in all the other allied fields, and soon had a reservoir of free-lancers drawn from the ranks and the staffs of the best publishers in New York. I had my pick when I needed them and could therefore pay them more than they were getting at their regular jobs.

For the first time in the history of subsidy publishing, the publisher received only letters of praise from writers. This I gambled on, since my books were better produced, better designed and actually published on schedule, a heretofore unheard-of procedure. It seemed that the more I gave to my authors the more business I did.

With the assurance and knowledge that I could get as many books to publish as I could possibly handle, I proceeded to lay the foundation for a systematic, economical, thorough promotion of books on a budget which would make most trade publishers laugh. I devised a new form of blurb for a jacket, using the same type for making a circular. This enabled me to get my circulars out at very little cost. In addition, I obtained the services of an excellent artist, and using standard patterns and designs, I never had to worry about the expense of designing book circulars; they fitted into predetermined patterns. Later on, I applied the formula to book jackets, and book design, and using basic designs could improvise typographical variations that gave my books a new look, without the conferences that consume staff time.

As the cost of publishing books increased, and the trade publisher needed to sell more and more copies to make a book profitable, more and more types of books, no matter how worth while, could be published only if subsidized. And I made the further discovery, which has become a backbone of my present business—that even when trade publishers are willing to consider "commission publishing," or "author participation," their prices and static formulas often put such publication out of an author's reach. My average book, in every respect as well printed and bound as trade books, costs the author about twelve dollars a page to be published. The trade publisher usually requires a minimum subsidy of thirty dollars a page because he has to publish larger editions. The number of our titles exceeds by many times that of the average trade publisher; and numerous time- and money-saving innovations I have made to keep costs down while keeping quality up are other major factors.

Today, Exposition Press is not only a subsidy publishing house but has three associated trade imprints. Besides a list of general books, we have a University imprint for scholarly texts at the college level, which compares with those of the university presses. We also have Exposition Banner Books, consisting of titles that have excellent long-term sales possibilities, and an Exposition–Lochinvar imprint under which we publish books dealing exclusively with the American West, an important area of Americana in which reader interest seems to be virtually unlimited.

Publishing, after all, presented no harder problems than learning how to walk again did. I have worked at it with the persistency with which I chinned and vaulted bars in a gymnasium as a kid, and later learned to pilot a boat in record time. The organization of a business establishment is very often the extension of the owner's make-up. I have surrounded myself with positive-minded personnel whose capacity for hard work is spiced with hearty good humor. I remember one associate in the early days, a southerner, who used to drawl whenever I gave him an assignment, "I'd gladly work myself to death for you, old man—but must it be tonight?" To this day I look for employees with a willingness to chuckle over their work.

Sometimes I have been forced to dramatize an issue to get it across to my suppliers. For instance, when one book was completed, the printer demanded a thousand dollars more than his initial estimate.

"Tom," I told him, "I have a quotation that says this book would cost me a thousand dollars less."

"Have you got it in writing?"

"No. I have your vice-president's word for it."

He shifted his strategy. "Look, what does a thousand dollars mean to a man like you?"

"Conceivably no more than it means to you."

"Well, it means nothing to me at all!"

I reached into my pocket and took out a half-dollar. I flipped it in the air, caught it and slapped it down on my desk.

"Tom, let's toss for a thousand dollars."

Greed glinted in his eyes as he gasped hopefully, "You mean if I win, you'll give me the thousand dollars?"

"No!" I replied. "Let's just toss for the grand."

White lines framed his lips as he said, "Whoever heard of tossing for so much money!"

"Why, Tom? Does it mean so much to you?"

"A thousand dollars is a lot of money!"

"All right. Since you've established that, I'll have to hold you to your estimate."

He saw the point and an impasse was averted.

The very heartbeat of our business has been enthusiasm for authors as human beings. The advantage to an author in publishing a book, even though it often doesn't return his investment in cash, is obvious. The publication of a book gives a writer authority and prestige. It may provide him with thousands of dollars' worth of publicity in his home town, and in the form of book reviews, news stories, and radio and television appearances. Book publication is an effective means of advancing in the business world, in the professions. In universities, publication often means promotion to a more desirable teaching post. *Who's Who in America* bristles with the books that this select coterie has published. I know, because many of the books published got them there. (Strangely enough, I made it the hard way, since this is my first book.)

Just as I have labored to retain the friendship of my business associates, I have worked to maintain the friendship of the reading public, even though I meet virtually none of them as individuals. For this reason we reject as many manuscripts as we publish. If a book is an evil book—and I would include in this category books by prosyletizing Communists, Fascists, warped religious fanatics—books that advance any socially destructive cause—I will not touch it. Only recently a biographer approached me about publishing a book on a bigoted American politician. He offered me substantial money. I am not in the position to turn away business gratuitously. Nevertheless, I felt that the acceptance of this manuscript would compromise my standards and I rejected it. A Fascist organization offered me $30,000 and a holiday in South America to publish the biography of Evita Perón, but turning that down was easy.

On the other hand, my list of publications has reflected every shade of healthy opinion. In the religious field, in a single season, I have published a novel by a rabbi, four books by Protestant ministers, short stories by a Catholic priest and a work by an outstanding scientist who took issue with the beliefs of organized religion.

In line with my policy of winning people to co-operate with me on every possible level, I have been careful to maintain good relations with the men and women associated with publicity media. With ten thousand books a year competing for newspaper and magazine space and for television and radio time, it requires ingenuity to obtain publicity for an author. Every publicity medium is exhaustively investigated by us. For instance, I have compiled a dossier on the literary preferences and idiosyncrasies of the many book reviewers. My appeal to their aesthetic vulnerabilities has effectively lubricated the wheels of publicity. My file on their tastes, I am certain, compares in thoroughness with the lists put together by the FBI for its own uses. And the result? My authors are delighted with the favorable fanfare that issues from these pens.

One of the reasons I have captured the imagination of my authors is that I permit them to work co-operatively with me at every stage of publication. It is astonishing how one can win the confidence of others by permitting them to share one's prerogatives. Upon signing a contract, I give the author a copy of the questionnaire that is filled out by our editorial staff for the purpose of evaluating a manuscript. The author is accorded the opportunity of appraising his own work from the objective standpoint of an editor. This experience gives him a new perspective on himself.

One author, with many successful books to his credit, wrote me recently: "For the first time, publishing a book is loads of fun."

In addition to the intangible satisfaction authors receive, there have been many concrete returns in dollars and cents for them. The author of one of our books wrote, "You may be interested in knowing that . . . several well-known businessmen contacted me after reading [my book] with the result that I have been able to earn substantial commissions from them for my services as a consultant."

Of course, no matter how friendly our business relations are, we, like all publishers, receive complaints from some authors. Over the years I have maintained a trouble-shooter to pour oil on troubled waters. After analyzing the tenor of complaints we discovered that they boiled down to one thing. Some authors simply refused to believe that the publisher was following through on all possibilities. If a book was not reviewed, they were sure this was because the publisher had forgotten to send out a review copy. If a bookstore did not order books, it was because the publisher had not contacted the store. If the local newspaper did not immediately send a reporter over with a cameraman, it was because the publisher had failed to inform the newspaper. If the local radio or TV station didn't invite the author to appear for a broadcast, the author shrieked "Sabotage!"

I have developed a system for narrowing down the area of friction insofar as it is humanly possible to do so. When a book is published, the author receives a list of sources to which the volume has gone for review, together with copies of the letters and releases that have been used to build publicity. As soon as we adopted this procedure, most of my authors wholeheartedly joined the game. They used my releases to establish their own personal contacts. I soon came to realize that my staff had developed into an organization of several hundred, each doing his utmost to plug titles in the field.

There are instances in the life of a business executive when his experience in human relations is put to the acid test. An author strode into my office and exploded, "Look here. My book has sold 1,850 copies. I have sold eighteen hundred and you have sold only fifty."

"That's splendid," I replied. "Five hundred more copies and the edition will be exhausted."

"Why can't *you* sell more copies?" he bellowed.

"Your book is of local interest. You are doing such a fine job in your community that there is absolutely nothing I can add to it."

This gentleman was completely mollified when I gave him an extra 10 per cent commission to show my appreciation for his sales efforts.

Exposition, more than any other publisher, attracts the grass roots. Chance plays a role in a number of our contacts. A postal clerk reading our sales circular in the mail may take his father's autobiography down from the shelf and send it in to us. A woman who has just moved into an apartment may receive one of our sales letters addressed to the previous occupant and unpack a volume of her own poetry. Once the waiter in a restaurant where I was dining overheard that I was a publisher and said to me, "I have a really 'hot' manuscript for you!" He brought it out from the kitchen, where it was lying under a heater in which the food was kept steaming!

Sometimes we have to reject the overtures of amateurs with genuine regret. And yet these instances occasionally develop an angle of humor.

Once while I was riding in a taxi, the cabbie, discovering I was a publisher, turned to me and said, "I've got a terrific book fer yuh. I wrote it myself—call it the *A Taxi Driver's Dilemma.*" I politely declined the opportunity to publish but expressed the hope that he could place the book elsewhere. "I'll be looking forward to seeing it in the bookstores."

"Oh, you won't know it's me what wrote da book," he explained. "I'm goin' to publish it ominously."

There are numerous other off-beat episodes, the marginalia of a publisher's life. At one time, a member of my staff was in his third year of Freudian analysis and his personality seemed to be retrogressing at an alarming rate. When his work began to deteriorate I started to check his correspondence carefully. Too late, I came across a letter he had written to one of my authors, a successful naturalist who had informed us he had two manuscripts, one on mountains and the other on caves. He wanted to know which manuscript we thought he ought to submit.

The letter my editor wrote him over my name gave me a jolt.

> DEAR SIR:
>
> It really doesn't matter which manuscript you submit since you know as well as I do that the mountain is nothing but a phallic symbol, and a cave is a vaginal symbol. And I guess they are both equally important.
>
> Sincerely yours . . .

I let my editor go with two weeks' pay. I felt that his prolonged analysis had led him irremediably back to his adolescence and that he could no longer do a man's job for me. Two months later I was in San Francisco, and one of the authors who wished to see me was the naturalist. After a few minutes of general conversation, I mentioned that I was aware of the letter my editor had written to him. Before I could apologize for its impertinence, he blurted, "Yes, I remember the letter. After discussing the implications very carefully with my analyst, I decided that the book I want to publish is the one on mountains!"

Occasionally in dealing with people I get the worst of the deal. One can't be infallible in feeling out the complex facets that make up the human personality. Once I was trimmed in a business deal and given a lot of trouble to boot when I signed a contract with a woman who had sent me a manuscript of verse, saturated with sweetness and light, with the Golden Rule theme predominant. She represented herself as the widow of an impoverished farmer, and knowing something of the sad conditions in her section of the country, I gave her what we dub in the office the "pauper's special," which ignores overhead but makes authors happy. Such books often lose us money but on the whole make us friends. This was an exception.

A few months after publication the writer's granddaughter came to New York loaded with complaints about my handling of the book. It had sold only 38 copies, despite the fact that we had mailed circulars to 1,300 friends. This was an insult to the author, seeing that she was so well known. . . .

At this point I got interested and by adroit questioning discovered that the "poor farmer's widow" owned 750,000 acres of good land leased to sharecroppers and that she was one of the least liked people in the state. She was indeed well known, so much so that she never stopped for the town's single traffic light because "three bankers and two mayors had been assassinated by disgruntled inhabitants while waiting for the red to turn green."

What's more, I learned that she wrote her poetry in between keeping her accounts and wrote both verse and accounts in the same ledger. The poetry was legible, the accounts, according to the tax collector, were not.

My life as a co-operative publisher was far from tranquil, but it was filled with variety and interest. I work hard, often from seven in the morning to after midnight. In building up a list of potential authors I still have to make long, tiring trips to various parts of the country because I like to meet my authors face to face.

My seat on the "left hand" of publishing—as well as my past interests in two trade-publishing firms—has led me to give much time and thought to the plight of the industry, and I have formed certain opinions and formulated several ideas which, given my long experience on the technical side of publishing, may be of interest.

Let's take these ideas of mine and rip them apart and see what they're worth.

CHAPTER V

After Spillane What?

The basic trouble with the publishing business is found in the publishers themselves, and to a lesser extent in certain leading writers: the assumption, fashionable these many years, that the intelligence and cultural quotients of Americans as a whole are low. A major result has been that publishers have never jointly promoted the cause of publishing among people who don't buy books; no attempt has been made to develop the vast potential market by *popularizing* the reading of books.

More than that, publishers seem to overlook the growing cultural awareness of the American masses—forgetting that from this source in each generation comes anew the public that booms Hi-Fi, fills our colleges and is the great audience of the better magazines and new quality paper-backs. It is here that the solution will be found, not in cultural societies and poetry circles, nor yet in scholarly dissertations in the weightier periodicals.

But let us take up first of all the assumption that hard-cover publishing is doomed. As far back as any of us can remember, Holy Rollers of the book world have been periodically prophesying that recreational interests would soon kill people's desire to read books since before 1900, when old Henry Holt was disturbed by the introduction of trolley cars, telephones and nickelodeons. At that time the fierce competition of the trolley car was "strangling" culture; yesterday it was the paper-back, today television. Tomorrow it may be round-trip excursions to the moon. But curiously enough, despite this periodic baking of the funeral meats, that stubborn old customer, the book-buyer, has refused to die.

Publishing has survived the nickelodeon and the bicycle built for two. It will, like music, survive even Liberace. Why should publishers be afraid of recreational diversions? Sex was introduced before literature, but the total reading hours of men and women has increased steadily over the years.

Failing to see the obvious solution of the intermittent crises, publishers and writers have laid the blame on America's fundamental lack of culture. One of the more pathetic exhibitions of our recent history has been the desertion of America by her top-flight authors. Henry James and T. S. Eliot became British subjects; Ezra Pound accepted the hospitality of France, subsequently betraying her when he found a more comforting domicile in Fascist Italy. Edith Wharton and Bret Harte lived permanently abroad. Ernest Hemingway went to Paris after World War I, ostensibly as the correspondent for a Canadian newspaper (although he was born a Middle Westerner) and remained there to join the American literati flooding the sidewalk cafés of Montparnasse, and at this writing prefers to make his home in Cuba. Sinclair Lewis died an exile in Florence, and today Paul Bowles lives in Tangier and Richard Wright in Paris.

All of them formed a concert to denounce the cultural standards of their fellow Americans.

In the 1920's, with Henry Mencken beating the drum, this Yankeephobia was exalted into a cult. Sinclair Lewis excoriated the American middle class and small-towner, and the word Babbitt entered the dictionary. Dos Passos, Fitzgerald and Cabell, among others, joined in the hooting. Through the literature of that decade ran a continual refrain:

America was an intellectual garbage dump and Europe was the matrix of culture. Out of this philosophy came *Main Street, Three Soldiers, The 42nd Parallel.*

A little later the new European culture took shape from Mussolini's hammering of the individual into the corporate state and from Adolf Hitler's burning of books and reducing millions of people, especially those with cultural or intellectual integrity, to soap and chimney smoke. At the moment when our rebel writers and *avant-garde* reviews were ridiculing and reviling American folkways, their opposite numbers in Europe were being herded into gas chambers—though a few, too few, escaped to add their luster to the American scene.

Belatedly there occurred a grand awakening, a realization of guilt on the part of our literati. But the damage had been done. The tradition that the average American is a cultural ape persists to this day. This conviction has been at the heart of publishing psychology, the source of its inhibitions and fears. Having no real faith in the intelligence of the public, publishers are hounded and harried by a continual sense of precariousness. They punctuate their scolding of the "ignorant little boy" with desperate attempts to win him over with spoon-fed pap.

The mentality of publishers is akin to the attitude of H. L. Mencken, who, in a classic thrust, said that the average man (the "booboisie," he called him) cannot grasp a bold new idea without being gradually prepared for it. If, declared Mencken, Darwin had printed his *Origin of Species* as a serial over a period of thirty years, he might have ended up being a member of the House of Lords or even becoming the Archbishop of Canterbury. But he gave the public an obliterative dose of evolution at one fell swoop and was damned for it as long as he lived.

It is true that our culture in many areas is geared to the mentality of adolescents. No one can deny that in our media of mass entertainment ideas are not wrestled but merely toyed with; that subjects cannot be dealt with in a way to arouse the basic fears, prejudices, disgusts of the audience. It is true that when Hollywood adapts a book for the screen, a corps of highly paid writers is detailed to extirpate whatever individual qualities have distinguished the manuscript, and so reduce the story to a stereotype. It is true that fornication cannot appear in the fiction of our popular magazines, although, as one editor put it, "no magazine can be held responsible for what happens between installments."

But these aberrations of popular taste are not a reflection on the intelligence of the American people; they are rather an indication of the cynicism of our idea merchants who, influenced by the dogmas of the literati, have acted in an arrogant and patronizing way toward the people. Americans are not so crass and stupid as the Hollywood Pooh-Bahs, the Madison Avenue hucksters, the slick editors apparently think. For decades Americans have been receiving arrows in their hides unprotestingly, and they have been permitting the sharpshooters to milk them of their kindness.

While Sinclair Lewis was thumbing his nose at American "Yahooism," his pockets were enriched by the very "provincials" he slandered, who bought his books in droves. Dos Passos and Cabell were lionized by the "ignoramuses" they insulted from their Olympian eyries.

No country has spent more money educating its youth in universities, endowing laboratories for scientific research, subsidizing intellectual refugees from Fascism and Communism. No people has lavished more money on art galleries, museums, libraries. Our "cultural wasteland" is dotted with more temples to art and learning than were ever seen anywhere in the history of the world. It is time that this be said.

Americans are a large-hearted race, as any down-trodden long-hair who has been picked from the gutter of European Bohemia and given a hundred-thousand-dollar-a-year job as a Hollywood director can testify. We are eager for new ideas. It is the mirthless merchandizers functioning as custodians of our culture who have betrayed us. They have betrayed Americans from the very level at which they learn to read.

Indeed, the perversion of children is a major industry. Children's fairy tales perform a psychologically useful function by transmuting the parent who is the instrument of authority into a witch, an ogre upon whom the child is permitted to act out his fantasy aggressions. But our contemporary merchants of ideas have carried this practice to an extreme. In children's comic books, for instance, violence is spoon-fed in lethal doses. Several hundred million comic books are sold yearly. Many children read at least a book a week. Assuming there is only one picture of violence a page, the child absorbs two hundred scenes of shooting, rape, arson, mass torture monthly. If he begins reading the comics at seven, by the time he is seventeen he has been indoctrinated with twenty-four thousand pictorialized shootings, stabbings and rapes.

These comics pay hypocritical lip service to law and order. They teach the reader (in their titles) that LAWBREAKERS —in caps—*are trapped by justice* (in small letters); that KIDNAPERS *always lose;* that MURDER *does not pay*. And the unctuous message gets across with a devastating impact. From the comics, juvenile criminals have found recipes for the poison they have fed to old women. They have committed burglaries, put bullets through their fathers' abdomens, and lynched their playmates according to a blueprint unfolded in cartoonist's ink.

The industry leaders shrug their shoulders in defending this cultural holocaust. "Business is business; if we don't print comics, somebody else will." Indeed, the hucksters who package their ideas for adults as well as children have been deliberately exploiting what psychologists have pointed out is a weakness in our national psychology. Americans are the only modern people who have massacred the original population of their country in modern times. Our sense of guilt has driven us to develop myth fantasies to which we have transferred our own motives of aggression—hence, for example, the celebrated "bad Injun" of our national fables, the good old Western proverb, "The only good Injun is a dead Injun," and others that no doubt come to mind. We had a guilt complex about the aggression of the West; our treatment and vilification of the Indian, the native American, has been self-justification.

But alas! The Indian now also goes to school. The Indian, believe it or not, pays taxes—and buys books, and sometimes writes them. The surviving Indians on our reservations have formed their own pressure groups, and now the wild-West films seen on TV have a new message: Not all Indians are bad!

Since Americans have a deep-rooted lust for violence—so runs the implicit rationalization of our hucksters—and since Americans are paranoid (viz., the Orson Welles broadcast of an invasion from Mars which panicked people from coast to coast), why not exploit this need for violence into big business? These gentlemen have unquestionably turned violence into the biggest business of our times. Our newspapers, movies, television and paper books hammer away at the theme. In fact, it is the opinion of many cynics that the chief reason millions of people are looking forward to color television is that they will be able to see the warm, dripping blood that appears over a prize fighter's eye in its natural red.

Certain interpreters of our folkways (for instance, the popular psychologists and "reputationed" educators on the payroll of the hucksters) maintain that this rechanneling of aggressive instincts through the media of picture magazines, TV thrillers and assorted trumpery is a healthy one. Is a man sexually impotent? Let him achieve his manhood by identifying himself with the bloodletting of Rocky Marciano in the prize ring. Weren't the Roman masses kept from breaking out in a revolution against the Caesars by being fed on a diet of bloody gladiatorial spectacles in the arena? Were not the Spanish people kept peaceful for centuries by a steady routine of bullfights?

It is especially interesting to me as a publisher to observe how the wise boys of my own medium have been participating of late in this shock therapy. The success of Mickey Spillane (an ex-comic-book-writer) is a prime example. In a Spillane story, the bacchanalian pleasures of sadism are varied by the tortured delights of masochism. Mike Hammer, Spillane's protagonist, is a homicidal paranoiac with all the characteristic tendencies of the disease. And like many paranoiacs he has a strong homosexual drive to commit deeds of violence.

It is against this nightmarish background of peddled violence that the fears of booksellers for the future can be assessed. The horns of the familiar dilemma pinion them. On the one hand, there is the deeply ingrained assumption that Americans are morons and have no taste for anything aesthetic, sensitive or subtle; on the other is the realization that the massive doses of violence to which the reader and the TV viewer is at present subjected may eventually desensitize him to such an extent that sensationalism will fail in its appeal.

There are only a limited number of positions in which a half-draped corpse may be posed for *True Detective*. The body has only so many organs to show (even if the post office were to remove all censorship). The breasts and genitals can be described only with a limited number of adjectives. Blood has but a single color. Already the four-letter words have been exhausted to such a point that authors are forced to invent new ones.

What will happen when the public has developed immunity to exhibitory vice? After Mickey Spillane—what?

Permit me to interject here my belief that the future of publishing is not nearly so black as some of the pundits have made out, because I disagree with the basic assumption that the American public consists in the mass of desensitized boobs and that the only way to part them from their dollars is to feed them a diet of bitch-heroines and he-virgins. We need only turn to the literature that has had the longest life in human history to realize that it has not been claque literature of the cultured few, but has been based on the most popular foundation conceivable. It is as old as the human heart, as rich as the human spirit. I refer to folk literature.

In their folk tales, Americans, since the days of the early pioneers, have traditionally found an outlet that channeled their fantasies into expressions of health, not perversity. Some of the sediment of folk literature has naturally been quite vulgar and spicy, because man has been eternally proud of his genital haberdashery. But the bulk and spirit of our folk literature has been material for greathearted achievements. An inspection of the all-time best-seller lists reveals, among other things, how commercially profitable it has been for writers and publishers to express themselves in a literature of folk symbols. Just to list some of the all-time favorites is to prove the point: *Tom Sawyer, Huckleberry Finn, Uncle Tom's Cabin, David Harum, The Hoosier Schoolmaster.*

There is excellent reason for the success of books written in the folk tradition. In every folk writer the child of long ago has lived with particular vividness in the adult self. In this literature, the child in the artist appeals directly to the child in the reader as well. Whatever else Mark Twain was, he was a child talking to other children and bringing them comfort in the night.

The sex and grue school of the present will never outsell the perennial classics of folk literature. As a matter of fact, not even the highly publicized snob writers have been able to achieve the solid popularity of the writers who have been in tune with the masses. If a literary historian of the future were to scan the list of over-all best sellers for the past hundred years, he might discover that the literary midgets of the past have outlived the literary giants of their day. He would learn that the authors who existed for the people were Harriet Beecher Stowe, Booth Tarkington, Mark Twain and Harold Bell Wright.

A number of the lesser "folk" writers had defects as artists. Edgar Rice Burroughs, although he displayed an extravagant imagination and a flair for storytelling, had a mediocre style. He had never been to Africa and knew nothing more about the locale of his Tarzan stories than what he had read in Stanley's *Darkest Africa.* Horatio Algier hardly wrote literature. (While indoctrinating millions of American youth with his formula for clean living, he had three illicit love affairs, one with a Paris grisette, one with an English art student and one with a married American woman.) Harold Bell Wright, a Rousseau of the Ozarks, was downright funny in some of his melodrama. (For instance, a teetotaler tramp who is starving refuses a saloon's offer of a tempting hot lunch because a glass of free beer was served with it.) For all their faults, however, these authors were constructive writers and their hold over the American people provides significant clues for today's publisher.

Indeed, a group of writers several notches above the Harold Bell Wrights were gathering the materials of new "folk" literature and following in their grass-roots tradition at the very time that Sinclair Lewis and company were bowing to the fanfares of the intelligentsia and H. L. Mencken and his satellites were searching the dictionary for new epithets of scorn. During the 1920's, while Lewis was ridiculing Gopher Prairie, Stephen Vincent Benét wrote his paean to American fortitude, *John Brown's Body;* while Edmund Wilson and Dos Passos were poking fun at American folkways, Carl Sandburg was glorifying the Chicago stockyards and Robert Frost was describing the dignity of the New England farmer. And not the least among these folk-tale spinners was Vachel Lindsay, who lived and worked among Americans of the backwoods, singing to them of Lincoln, Jackson, P. T. Barnum and their other heroes. Like Whitman, he wrote of the common people not only as they were, but as they might become.

Of all this group of writers, Carl Sandburg best typifies the way to the salvation of American literary culture. He is the prototype of the writer whom publishers must recruit if the book-buying public is to withstand the assaults of Mike Hammer. Sandburg knows American life intimately because he has played so many roles in it. Unlike the rootless Left Bank intellectuals who, for the most part, knew the America they despised only prophylactically, Sandburg has been a cook, a roustabout, the secretary to the mayor of Milwaukee. He has driven a milk wagon, worked in a barbershop, served as a scene shifter in a theater, as a truck handler in a brickyard, a dishwasher, a harvest hand, a carpenter's helper. At one period he went from door to door with a pot of blacking in his hands, offering to polish stoves in exchange for meals. Here *is* a man who has suffered more fully than any of the sophomoric cynics who have created their nihilistic Mike Hammers. And yet he has never lost faith in the common man.

He saw poetry where no one had ever seen it before—in the skyscrapers and motorcars, the railway engines and tractors and slaughterhouses of America. In his writing he uses picture words as the early American Indians used them; his blood warms to the smoke and steel, the rich black loam, the smells of the slums. Eschewing the princes and princesses of the European fairy tale, he wrote a book of fairy tales for children using the symbols and idioms of the New World. He spun yarns about finding a Zigzag Railroad, a Village of Liver-and-Onions, The Village of Cream-Puffs. He created such characters as Hot Dog the tiger, Poker Face the baboon, and Jason Squiff whose hat, shoes and mittens were made of popcorn.

When this American troubadour wrote an epochal biography of Lincoln, he felt so spiritually akin to his subject that there are quotations from Lincoln in the text that might well have been spoken by Sandburg, and lines of Sandburg that could have come from Lincoln. *The People, Yes,* is the title of one of Sandburg's volumes of poetry. This is the creed by which he lives and works.

Today American culture has reached the crossroads. A Carl Sandburg, the Pied Piper of our folk literature, represents the spiritually fructifying elements in our culture. Perhaps the person who most skillfully represents the negative, nihilistic elements, of which the comic books, the sex and grue private eye, the pulp cult of violence form the lowest base, is Ernest Hemingway. Like Sandburg, Hemingway is more than an artist; he is a symbol.

Just as Sandburg affirms the dignity of the little fellow, so Hemingway, the high priest of the intelligentsia, denies it. Just as Sandburg has remained spiritually bonded to the prairies, Hemingway exiled himself from them after his strictly American boyhood in the Middle West. When he speaks at all affectionately about a people, it is the Spanish bullfighters, a group of primitives who are functionally remote enough from civilization to strike a responsive chord in him. Just as his life has been a prolonged escape from his origins, so too has his writing. Although it has been called the literature of realism, it is actually a literature of escape.

As a matter of fact, Hemingway has become the slave of the escapist legend projected by his admirers. In the role of the intellectual's Superman, he rushes off to Africa to kill lions. He lives a life of tailormade violence whetting the imagination of the secluded intellectual even as Lord Byron did before him. He is the *Übermensch,* on a higher level than Spillane's Mike Hammer; but they are essentially blood brothers: all of Hemingway's skill and virtuosity cannot conceal this fact.

So we are here at the crossroads again: Will our cultural future be dominated by the philosophy of the Sandburgs or by that of the Hemingways? Will the future belong to our folklore or to the cult of violence?

Today the lifespan is greater than ever. Millions of Americans who have retired from jobs and businesses and who have been freed from the responsibilities of child-rearing have been given a new leisure. Not only people over fifty, but everyone who lives in this perplexing world of today, is eager for information, interpretation, guidance that good books can contribute. Never before have publishers had so vast an audience of people waiting to be reached by the written word and educated in the enduring values of our civilization. Furthermore, never before have we had so many literate writers who have mastered the techniques of their craft and are equipped to communicate with the American people. We publishers have the materials in hand for a tremendous expansion of our business if only we could be convinced of it and guided by our convictions.

By all means let us preserve the technical excellence of our Hemingways who have mastered the primitive rhythms of language; but let us infuse it with a soul. Let us pour the best of our folk literature into the streamlined mold of our modern literary technology. When we have successfully joined the power of *The Sun Also Rises* with the vital fantasy of *L'il Abner* to produce the Great American Novel of the future, we need never again fear that any diversionary force will be able to vanquish the written word.

CHAPTER VI

Who Will Buy My Books?

Publishers are the only businessmen in America who, as a class, make no concerted effort to improve their sales, the only businessmen who will spend thousands of dollars producing an article and then sit on their hands hoping that someone will find out about it and buy it. Why? Well, before we consider the peculiar psychology of publishers, let's set down a few facts and a few ideas and see where they lead us.

If trade publishing is today reaping the harvest of shortsightedness, narrow-mindedness and inefficiency, how did these faults come about? I was proud when a prim editor dubbed me "the rogue of Publishers' Row." But when the book industry as a whole suffers, so do I. And so do my authors. On their behalf if not on my own let's look into this thing.

At present there are (as we said in the beginning) close to a million Americans suffering from writer's itch. About ten thousand of these are professional free-lances who supply the book, magazine, movie and radio and television markets. Of these the group with a perpetual heartache is that of the writers of books.

As stated before, each year eleven thousand books are published, and of these perhaps a few hundred reach sales of ten thousand copies or more. According to present royalty scales, ten thousand copies of a book sold will pay the author $4,000 in royalties. This means that only a small handful of writers are able to live on the earnings of their books. More than half the writers registered with the Authors' League of America earn under $3,000 a year.

Yet despite this crushing economic picture for professionals, thousands of tyros sit down monthly to write or dictate the Great American Novel, confident that it will bring them riches and undying fame. Writing is a talent which a few are born with and a craft which takes years of experience to learn. Few writers can learn by themselves. They must learn as they work, as is the case in any trade, and they must be helped by editors. Who among trade publishers is helping the authors of tomorrow, today?

There are a few writers who establish themselves quickly more through luck than talent, and others who understand publicity better than they do writing. Do you know anyone who knows a friend who has a relative who knows Walter Winchell? One line in a Winchell broadcast can sell certain books better than a weekly mention for a year in the *Saturday Review*. Why? Because Winchell is heard and believed by the multitude and the *Saturday Review* is read by the critical few. Most of the periodicals read by people do not contain book reviews.

As to the successful professionals, most of them make their real incomes from television, radio, movies or advertising, and only their incidental pin money from books. But books alone mean *prestige*.

No matter how many four-letter words the literati use in their writings, they are considered respectable enough to address women's literary *soirées*. Although many of them have no genuine culture, according to the standards of literary gentlemen of previous ages, a few of them are touched with genius. Historically, the serious writer has been at odds with his environment. Our contemporary "white hopes" of literature are the first as a group to have turned an artistic somersault and landed in complete alignment with the times. Instead of rebelling against the mood of society, they have flattened themselves into conformity with it. In an age of assembly-line specialization, they specialize along with everyone else.

Our young literati don't write about life in large letters—only about a fragment of life. If they've been to war, they write one novel about that and vanish into the lush cocoon of Hollywood. They know man only as a fragment—the Freudian man, the economic man, the sociological man. A few writers have become the world's foremost specialists in fictionalized homosexuality. If they follow up their first novel with a second, third or tenth, it is usually about their own adolescent discovery of sex in a hayloft. They shrink from dealing with adult realities of the world we live in—Russia, the H-Bomb, the dollarocracy of our society. Refraining from developing themes on the vast canvases that gave Balzac, Tolstoy, Dostoyevsky their catholicity, our modern writers exhaustively examine the cobwebs in the attic of a ruined southern mansion. It is easier to remain a specialist, secure in one's mastery of a fragment of life.

It is this premium our society places on specialization that has dehydrated the nonfiction as well as the fiction writing of our times and makes free-lance authorship an especially hazardous occupation for the neophyte to enter. If the writer tries to peddle articles to the top magazines, he will find that in most cases only the specialist is given a hearing. Indeed, he will discover that slick nonfiction magazines like *Life* and *Fortune* cultivate a large staff of research specialists who know nothing about writing, and a stable of writers who know nothing about research. The finished article is simply a welding together of the two groups. The benighted free-lance, that individual artist with his idiosyncratic style, is clearly at a disadvantage and the essayist, the man of letters grounded in the nineteenth-century humanities, is an anachronism.

Indeed, as one of these anachronisms, Joseph Wood Krutch, has remarked, it would seem that the magazine writing in demand today could most efficiently be produced by an electronic brain. "Perhaps, in time, it will actually be produced that way, since such machines now solve differential equations; and that is harder to do than write the average magazine article." If Vannevar Bush were to put his mind to it, he might well replace the entire list of editors, assistant editors and researchers employed by Henry Luce with an electronic machine less complicated than the one now used to estimate the path of an atomic missile head.

The free-lance magazine or book writer today cannot sell himself as a simple fellow who has a homespun message for readers. He must be an authority on a subject. He must have a cure-all for the physical or mental ills that beset us, or a solution for world-shaking political problems (or, at the very least, he must have run off with a Hollywood actress and made Earl Wilson's column as a specialist in wife-stealing). The American public often must be presold on a writer before they'll read him in large numbers.

The odds against a man's earning much more than cigarette money are even more overwhelming for a book writer than for a general free-lance; for whatever readers there are for the printed word have largely been siphoned off over the last fifty years by the mass-circulation magazines. It takes a little more time to read a book than the average subway rider is willing to spend. *Reader's Digest* was created to serve the millions of subway denizens who were too busy to read even a magazine.

In tune with this literary crusade to oversimplify knowledge, our culture is dedicated to glorifying youth. This campaign is motivated by economics. Young people remain customers for deodorants, toothpastes and cheeses longer than the middle-aged and the aged. So, by a psychological sleight-of-hand, all consumers—young, middle-aged and elderly—are lumped together into the role of the stereotyped teen-ager. "Keep that schoolgirl complexion," cosmetic advertisers tell millions of elderly harridans and leathery-faced beldames of forty. Romance on television and in magazines is pictured in glowing, youthful terms, provoking the menopausal grocer's wife with grown-up grandchildren into sighing for her lost adolescence. The bewildered consumer who yearns to be permitted to grow up is confronted with a grabbag of gadgets designed not to make life more intellectually or emotionally satisfying, but simply to make it *easier* for him. Young honeymooners are bombarded with propaganda that they have entered a career not of homemaking but of playing house—"and won't you buy our new refrigerator, washing machine, electric mixer for your little dollhouse?"

For a generation the movies have been concocting fraudulent fantasies of perpetual adolescence. They have done it so flagrantly that they have finally succeeded in driving away millions of adults from the box office. In fact, recent statistics indicate that Hollywood has remained solvent only because of the accident of a rising birth rate that pours new shock troops of teen-age fodder into the movie houses as fast as the adults depart.

The day will yet come when millions of patiently enduring Americans will suffer an emotional blowout that may send our civilization spinning. Adults, no matter how intelligent, *do* undergo a process of maturing emotionally through the experiences of marrying, raising children, losing dear ones through death. This inevitable exposure to suffering places a gulf between adult and the world of the adolescent.

Our culture is not filling the emotional needs of the American adult. The teen-ager becomes a casualty as well. After being fed on a diet of false values, he is suddenly confronted, upon entering adulthood, with a series of psychological shocks for which he is totally unprepared. The truths about adult life do not correspond to the promises our culture has made to him. There has been no preparation for adjustment. Society will yet pay the price for the promises it has broken, the faith it has failed to keep with its young. It is rearing a citizenry that will punish it for its failure to be honest.

In the meantime, the harassed writer, who is theoretically dedicated to interpreting society honestly, is caught between Scylla and Charybdis. Should he support the organized lies of the group, hold up a deliberately distorted mirror to his public and earn a living as a peddler of literary opiates, or should he reveal the facts, stripped of their illusion, and be howled down as an apostate?

A by-product of this cultural saturnalia dedicated to adolescence is the periodic attack made on intellectuals by mobs of know-nothings led by the McCarthys and other right-wingers. The thinker is ridiculed as an "egghead." All organs of propaganda are united in their campaign to discredit the intellectual. In the movies, the college professor is continually characterized as an absent-minded fool; he is the butt of all the jibes; the scientist is represented as an insane mastermind plotting to blow up the world with a secret formula.

It is an inevitable step from discrediting the intellectual in the movies to driving him out of the State Department, browbeating him before congressional committees of investigation, banning his books from government-sponsored libraries.

The irony is that our civilization is founded foursquare upon the achievements of the intellectual. American heavy industry is vitally dependent on scientific research; higher education is becoming increasingly a *sine qua non* for the top jobs in our economy. The attack on the trained mind is completely outdated by realities.

In any event, the writer, who usually cherishes the unfashionable procedure of growing up and who may even be guilty of doing a little thinking himself at times, can be a maladjusted individual living in a nation of Peter Pans.

I do not know whether the strains and stresses of their occupation have turned many writers into cynics, driven them to drink, scrambled their personal lives; but I suspect that some of the fraternity wear schizophrenia as a badge of merit. Some writers of the tenderest love stories can't stay attached to a spouse long enough to complete the installments on the refrigerator. One well-known psychologist who imparted to millions the secret for staying happily married divorced his third wife after his book had reached the best-seller lists.

Like a bull in a china shop the harassed writer frequently swipes at everything within his reach; and this includes virtually everyone connected with the book industry. A favorite strawman—the booby-trapper, many writers are convinced, is out to spill their blood—is the literary critic. To the average author, whose paranoia dates if not from birth at least from the arrival of his first meager royalty statement, the villain responsible for the poor sale of *The Life and Times of a Water Tick* is the critic who ignored the book or wrote an unfavorable review of it. There are genteel elderly authors, lifelong antivivisectionists and squirrel watchers, who if they met Edmund Wilson, Clifton Fadiman or Orville Prescott in a dark alley would strangle them while chuckling hideously.

The actual truth, of course, is that literary critics have small influence either with Beelzebub or the Archangel Michael in sending an author to hell or heaven. Occasionally an Alexander Woollcott will launch the career of a James Hilton, or a William Lyon Phelps will lean on his mashie at the sixteenth hole and issue a pronunciamento that will bring a Thornton Wilder riches and glory, but the average book reviewer is in a different category.

The reviewer, as distinct from the literary critic—and there is a very strong distinction—may be a staff man called "literary editor" who writes a daily or weekly column of book reviews. Or he may be a reporter for a newspaper whose editor distributes books for review indiscriminately among the staff. Or he may be a specialist, such as a garden editor, who habitually comments on books in his sphere. There are syndicated columns of book reviews (the bane of an author, since he will receive twenty clippings from his clipping agency all identical and for all of which he must pay) and there are free-lance reviewers who work for small-town newspapers in return for the review copies, which they sell to local bookstores.

There was a time not far distant when a book reviewer was the least-paid scrivener on a paper's staff, a hard-working writer who earned his tiny wage by gorging himself on a diet of sawdust to find an occasional plum. The wage has gone up because of the activities of the American Newspaper Guild, which insists that a newspaperman be paid according to his length of service rather than his talent. Some literary critics now receive almost as much as a star reporter.

The reviewers are divided by publishers into grades. Grade A reviewers, those on big city newspapers and important magazines, receive well before publication the most important books on the list. They may receive as many as two thousand books a year—all of which, if they are conscientious, they have to read. (And here I may say that in my experience a good reviewer—and they are many—skimps his work no more than a good mechanic or a good doctor.)

At the same time, a practiced reviewer will not read every word of every book he reviews; to do so he would have to read half a dozen books a day. We have found that he appreciates being given a summary of what the book is about, well in advance of its receipt. When he receives the book he will be eager or not, as the case may be, to read it with care. Some reviewers have their pet subject—the late Joseph Henry Jackson of the San Francisco *Chronicle* was meticulous in his coverage of Western Americana. Newspapers like the New York *Times,* the *Herald-Tribune,* the Chicago *Tribune* or the Kansas City *Star* have specialists in various subjects on whom they call.

The gulf between reviewing and literary criticism is wide, as has been delicately admitted by Clifton Fadiman, who is a critic. The work of the Drydens, the Hunekers, the Beerbohms, the Taines and the Shaws goes far beyond the province of reviewing; sometimes, indeed, the book is fortunate to be mentioned in connection with the critic's own more important views. But while some contemporary book reviewers have never written a line of valid criticism in their lives, they are extremely important to the author: their work is read in the local bookstores, and book buyers and reorders may be the result.

To understand the book reviewer is to excuse his occasional lapses. He may have conned ten thousand books over a decade and be a little punch-drunk. To be capable of opening the latest historical novel with fresh interest after all the tripe he has plodded through since *Gone With the Wind,* the reviewer must bring to his work a perpetual mental chastity which can be obtained only by forgetting a book as soon as he has written the review. After two years as literary editor of the San Francisco *News,* Basil Woon gave up reading books in order to continue writing them and was so sickened by books in general that he gave away his entire library. But the reviewer who sticks to his job must—in the happy phrase of Clifton Fadiman—retain "his surprisability"; he must never even hint at how bored he really is.

It is obvious that the job of a reviewer is not an easy one and requires important aptitudes. One of the characteristics that frequently disqualifies a man, however, is creative talent. The fellow who itches to write creatively instead of reflecting the muse as the moon borrows light from the sun should often apply elsewhere. The successful book reviewer is the kind of individual who, although he sucks at the paps of literature for a lifetime, has little more chance of becoming an author than an elephant has of flying.

Nevertheless, this hard-working journeyman does not deserve to be badgered or held up to ridicule by writers. In many cases he is doing a more honest day's work than they are. Far from sinking his darts often enough into the writer's hide, the reviewer is too charitable toward the sewage that seeps out of publishing factories. He is a chronic optimist who seems determined to hunt out the least sliver of good in the worst of writing and to preserve an amiable tolerance toward fools.

One thing might be said by way of qualification for the writer: while he uses the book reviewer as a convenient scapegoat, the number-one whipping boy in his stable is somebody else. The chief scoundrel in his gallery of bogeymen, the individual at whose doorstep the writer lays all the evils of this world, is the book publisher. Most writers seem convinced that a publisher is a fellow who drinks champagne out of an author's skull. Publishers have been accused of picking an author's brain, beating him down to sweatshop royalties, conspiring with booksellers to keep his books hidden under the counter and juggling his royalty statement. Many writers would be amazed if told that publishers are honorable human beings, and that if you prick them with a pin, they bleed blood.

If the average writer cannot earn the income of the drugstore clerk, the trouble is indicated in statistics beyond the control of any single publisher. The industry as a whole is sick. Americans spend twenty times as much money on sporting equipment (golf clubs, fishing tackle, motorboats, hunting rifles) than on books. The situation today is not so bad as back in the 1920's, when Governor Al Smith made the deathless observation, "Where in the hell would I *go* to buy a book?" But the fact remains that the machinery for distributing trade books still smacks of the days of the village blacksmith. While a community of a thousand people can support a movie house, it takes fifty thousand people to support a bookstore. Of the four-thousand-odd bookstores in the United States, the majority are concentrated within five hundred miles of New York City.

Publishing is no stronger than the weakest link in its distribution chain. Among the fifteen hundred publishing firms in the nation, only one hundred do a business of more than $100,000 annually. The majority of houses are smaller than the typical New York City law firm. A book bought by less than one per cent of the population can be considered a sensational best-seller.

Publishing operates on principles that would drive other manufacturers crazy. The raw material is the unpredictable brain of the author who may or may not meet his deadline and whose output is of an uncertain quality. Unlike other manufacturers who progressively reduce the price of their product to move it off the counters, the publisher takes a complete loss if he cannot sell his goods at the original price. Most of his products don't come to the attention of enough potential purchasers to make his investment worth while.

Though publishers would like to conduct themselves along the lines of the average manufacturer, the merchandising problems of a publisher are vastly more intricate than those of the typical manufacturer. During the course of a year, several publishers issue more than two hundred books each, or an average of one for every business day. Each book is a unique product with its own individual problems. If a cosmetic manufacturer had to issue and plan the merchandising of a brand-new product every business day, he would throw up his hands. Yet, in spite of the peculiar problems of the book industry, some of its merchant princes have deluded themselves into the belief that they are selling just another variety of soap, instead of realizing that their problem is not to sell a *product* but an *idea.*

When publishers first put their books into drugstores, in the 1930's, Ellis Parker Butler, the humorist, was moved to write cynically that this should relieve the publisher of much of the mental worry he had previously had in selecting book manuscripts; now he could turn that work over to a committee of drugstore clerks. A clerk could notify the publisher, for instance, that only 16 per cent of his customers bought books last month and that the next lot of novels should be slanted more strongly for the users of Hair-Glosso; or he could recommend that more of Ezekiel Snipe's books should be reissued, for they were going well with the humidor and briar-pipe trade.

Authors and booksellers often remark about the reluctance of publishers to provide the trade journals with statistics of profits and losses. This reluctance is due not to any inborn secretiveness or dishonesty, but simply to shame. In a nation of efficient business where invested capital expects to receive a minimum return of 6 per cent and more, book publishers feel understandably sheepish about expending their energies in an industry that, if it provides any profit at all, returns as little as one per cent and averages 3 per cent at the most.

An effort has been made by publishers within the last twenty-five years to circumvent the bottleneck of the bookstore and to aim at every home the postman calls at. The book clubs have, by previous publishing standards, developed mass markets. They have pumped new blood into the arteries of the industry, and have represented the only major advance in the merchandising of hard-cover books since the Spanish-American War. Nevertheless, the impact on the American economy of even the book club can be judged by the fact that, not long ago, the stock of the Book-of-the-Month Club (the second largest club), when finally it was put on the exchange, was traded at the sluggish rate of two to three hundred shares a day at ten dollars a share.

Yet the clubs are the only segment of the industry in tune with the general tempo of American merchandising. Like the hucksters in allied fields—the promoters of mass-circulation magazines, for instance—they have learned the value of serving culture in a predigested form akin to Clapps baby food. This practice of grinding facts into pap has reached such a point that the Book-of-the-Month's publicity department spares the ladies of literary clubs the trouble of reading the books they report on to their audiences; the club sends out, free, delightfully packaged book reviews written in basic English which the reviewer can transmit verbatim to her intellectual satellites. And the club did more. It issued a syndicated column for eight hundred newspapers which, in the fashion of Bob Ripley's Believe-It-or-Not, publicized quaint, piquant facts about literature to whet the appetite of the adult teen-ager.

True to its multi-faceted concept of integrity, the Book-of-the-Month has managed to keep its skirts clear of political issues. On one occasion, when it seemed it might have to surrender its status as an intellectual Janus, it solved the problem neatly by serving up as a dual selection Herbert Hoover's *Challenge to Liberty* and Henry Wallace's *New Frontiers,* thus preserving its integrity. Despite the eclectic literary tastes of its board of judges, it must be confessed that the boys have been guilty of some grievous errors of judgment. Hemingway was overlooked by them until *For Whom the Bell Tolls;* Faulkner was ignored until he won the Nobel prize. Thomas Wolfe was never "discovered" by the Book-of-the-Month judges.

To many a book writer, already bristling with resentment against publishers, critics and booksellers, the book clubs are another bête noire. Authors think it unfair that the clubs should focus the spotlight upon a few books arbitrarily and promote them into mammoth successes. They feel that since there is only a limited amount of public tolerance for books at best, to drain off the lion's share for a few deprives the many of even the moderate sales they might expect if all publications were forced to scramble for recognition. Writers contend that it would be more equitable if the clubs selected half a dozen books a month, for 25,000 sales apiece, instead of handing the plum of 150,000 sales or more to one full-busted volume.

It is significant, however, that current club procedures are vital to their success. In line with other branches of successful merchandising, they standardize their output and mass-produce it. This is in direct contradiction to trade-publishing practices. Indeed, one of the criticisms of trade publishers has been that they continue to expand their lists, loading them with books that can never be merchandised properly whereas they would be better off if they concentrated on a few titles and plugged away for increased sales on these.

Down in the bargain basement of the publishing industry a new operation has recently mushroomed—the paper-backed books that provide kudos for some writers. In a good business year, over 900 paper-book titles are issued, about 230,000,000 copies are sold; and about $4,000,000 in royalties is distributed to authors.

At first glance it looks as though a lush new outlet has been opened for the book author. However, there are definite reservations to be noted. The majority of the nine leading companies in the industry are magazine, not trade-book houses; and many authors who benefit most are alumni from the pulps. It should be noted, however, that certain paper-book houses, notably Penguin, Vintage, Signet and Anchor books, in contradistinction to the main trend of the industry, have successfully merchandised literary classics. Unfortunately, the worthless titles still overwhelmingly outnumber the worth-while ones and the impact of the industry as a whole remains, in my opinion, an unwholesome one.

People in the industry point with pride to their whizz-bang merchandising accomplishment; but much of their satisfaction is premature. After half a dozen years of a wildcat boom, the operators have come perilously close to saturating their market. Having offered the consumer all the lust and killing he can stomach, the industry is being forced into a reappraisal of its aims. The majority of "big bid" reprints (for which $15,000 or more is offered the trade publisher) do not recoup their guarantees. Although the industry has 100,000 retail outlets, fewer than 70,000 sell with any real effectiveness. Over 80 per cent of the total sales come from less than one-third of the dealers. While paper-back books have been selling about 230,-000,000 copies a year, magazines sell annually over 3,500,-000,000 copies. A single magazine, *Life,* sells more copies in twelve months than the total output of the paper-book industry. The success of paper books hasn't altered the fact that although Americans read more than any other people in the world, they still do the bulk of their reading in periodicals and comic books.

The big weakness of the paper-book industry lies in its method of distribution. The books are handled by magazine distributors as though they were magazines. The life of a magazine on the dealer's stand is less than a month. If it doesn't sell, it is returned to the publisher. The dealers treat paper books in the same fashion. As a result, titles become outdated in a matter of weeks. The average writer's appearance is almost as brief as that of the mayfly. Very few buyers, even if they enter a drugstore with a particular title in mind, will take the trouble to go from one store to another hunting for it. They will grab whatever is at hand. The publisher finds himself loaded with valuable backlist items that he cannot make available to the public in large enough quantities. Few of his best-selling titles are on the stands at one time. Until the bulk of dealers divorce their book distribution from their magazine distribution and hire employees who are primarily concerned with books, tremendous potential sales will continue to be lost by the industry.

At present, the paper-covered volume, forced into competition with magazines, is neither fish, flesh nor fowl. One publisher has called it the "bookazine." To hold its own with the *Police Gazette, Beauty Parade* and sex-hygiene magazines, it has been forced to sport some lurid covers which make it look like a house organ for the white-slave industry.

It may comfort parents and senatorial investigating committees to know that the American people have successfully survived previous outbreaks of paper books. As far back as the 1880's, dime novels and paper reprints were turned out in such quantities that publishers reached the saturation point in profits. They were stuck with huge unsold stock. One bookseller, in a mood reminiscent of the fraternity today, complained, "These books are everywhere. They are hawked on the streets; they crowd the El stations . . . I am conscious of a feeling of nausea at the mere sight of the paper-backs."

Whether the paper-book publishers of today will constipate the goose that lays the golden eggs remains to be seen. At any rate, writers who have been forced to take smaller advances as a result of the industry's recent entrenchment know that the battle for survival is on.

Looking at the publishing picture as a whole, one can understand why the majority of book writers live in economic peonage and why publishers count their profits—when they earn them—in the thousands, not the millions. The book industry is continually plagued by a paradox. There are fewer readers for serious books in the United States in relation to its population than in any other civilized nation in the Western world. Yet, as we said, Americans read more printed matter (magazines, newspapers, comic books) than any other people.

The guts of any industry are its distribution system; publishing distribution has been a disgrace for a hundred years. There are close to two million retail stores in the United States and of these only four thousand or so are real retail book outlets. Twenty-five hundred of these are insignificant in size; an additional thousand do not carry a comprehensive stock. Less than five hundred serious book outlets are available for satisfying the needs of one hundred and sixty-six million Americans!

Bookselling is a time-honored business. Indeed, in ancient Egypt booksellers had stalls at the entrance to the Pyramids. They sold the mourners (who were concerned with what the dead would do with their leisure) inscribed tablets to be buried along with food and other household belongings. Some volumes booksellers hawk today also seem to have been written for the dead.

Virtually year after year, the number of booksellers who go bankrupt is greater than the number of booksellers who enter the business. Most booksellers obtain their major business from their greeting-cards and stationery sections. If they depended upon the return from books they would soon go broke. The "successful" bookseller's profit on books, after taxes, averages in "good" years three-quarters of one per cent!

All this is common knowledge in the trade. But the greatest disgrace of all is that publishing houses who depend so vitally upon their distribution outlets have done virtually nothing as a group to help the bookseller in his plight. No other responsible manufacturer has ever been guilty of such epic indifference. For instance, recently the pharmaceutical industry faced a crisis because of the unstable condition of its retail trade, indicated by the rash of bargain sales in drugstores engaged in cutthroat competition. The drug manufacturers immediately got together and devised a program to enable the individual drugstore to survive without engaging in destructive price-cutting tactics.

Far from making a concerted effort to assist the harassed bookseller, publishers go blandly, selfishly about their business instituting policies that in many cases actually weaken him. It is a legitimate question how long the book business, basically a retail business, can continue to operate this side of bankruptcy if it continues to undermine the retail outlets upon which its well-being depends.

There are, of course, ways in which the bookseller can help himself to develop a more efficient operation. Booksellers should make a special effort to secure a better class of employees with a promise of job tenure. Instead of taking on the odd-job buffo—the high school hoyden who puts together the change she makes as a salesgirl with her baby-sitting earnings to buy a new dress—or the white-collar loafer who is a master at sleeping on his feet with his mouth open, booksellers should hire men and women who have a kinship with the books they sell.

In this connection publishers may one day see the light and actually send out sales experts to train bookstore personnel in the techniques of book promotion. Perhaps publishers might set up sales clinics to indoctrinate the bookseller in the successful procedures that are par in other branches of retailing. After all, there's a $40 profit in every $100 worth of books sold.

In the meantime, booksellers might well follow the procedure established by Adolph Kroch, who founded one of the most successful stores in the country and whose test for buying each volume was whether a reader could be found to fit it. Other successful booksellers have tabulated a list of their clients according to vocation, hobbies, tastes and continually send out letters offering books that fit the individual. No book is buried on the shelf without being thoroughly exploited to see whether it can match a prospective buyer. Window displays are a vivid reflection of the literary and social trends current in the community.

One possible way to increase store sales would be for the industry to run a nation-wide publicity and advertising campaign geared to make America more book-conscious. Other industries have had excellent success with mass indoctrination for their products; it is high time that book people use these high-powered tools of propaganda.

The futility of bookselling becomes apparent at the annual convention of the American Booksellers' Association. Booksellers are wined and dined, and salesmen spend more time signing expense vouchers than they do writing orders. At a recent convention, I was almost annihilated when I offered to bet that I could get every bookseller to visit my booth and order at least one book. The gimmick was simple. All I wanted was a six-foot redheaded "historical fiction" type model to run a dice "birdcage" in the booth. On his order the bookseller would get a discount of 40 per cent plus whatever numbers came up on the cubes. The boys at my table were horrified. "It lacks dignity." "It would get the convention raided and make tabloid news." "This is *not* the way to sell books." I discarded the approval implied in these remarks, because, unfortunately, the booth next to mine was that of a Bible publisher. So I've let that idea go . . . I think.

But here's another idea for the industry, and it can't fail so long as human nature prevails. Industries, professions and even abstract virtues are commemorated in Eat-an-Apple Week, Be-Kind-to-Your-Kidneys Day, not to mention Valentine Day and Mother's Day, which was successfully promoted for the benefit of florists and candy merchants. For booksellers I suggest Bygones Day, a day each year when all resolve to "forgive and forget, and let bygones be bygones." You send an appropriate book, inscribed on the flyleaf, to everyone you would like to say "sorry" to. Lives there a person who does not regret at least one impulsive or unkind action that he'd like to atone for—if it weren't too embarrassing or troublesome? I suggest that the booksellers promote this day, before the liquor industry picks it up.

Every small town in America has cultured elderly ladies and learned gentlemen who dwell in genteel—and lonely—poverty and would love to make a few extra dollars a week. All they need do is to convert the spare room to a literary center and nicknacketeria by stocking it with books, and using it as a meeting place for the local poets or writers' group, and they would sell books. Certainly books that now gather dust in publishers' warehouses would soon have owners, and incidentally serve as a much-needed tax deduction or business expense for these people who usually live on tiny, tax-plagued incomes.

Through the medium of book reviews, the publishing industry is continually obtaining free publicity—more than that obtained by virtually any other industry. But, as in the case with booksellers, the publishers have made no concerted effort to encourage this medium of book publicity; indeed, they have done their best—unwittingly—to make a book magazine's life as difficult as possible.

Time and again the editors of the *Saturday Review* and other influential publications have pleaded with publishers to space the release of their books in a more orderly fashion than at present. As matters now stand, important books are published en masse during several key months of the year (April, May, October, November). The book reviewer cannot possibly handle all the titles that merit attention. A large number of them must be reluctantly neglected. If the leading books on a publisher's list were spread out in their release over the year, instead of being bunched during several weeks of the spring and fall seasons, much of the confusion that today characterizes book-reviewing practices would be cleared up. Furthermore, it would pay for publishers to abandon their obsessive secretiveness and get together with one another to release a co-ordinated schedule of important books to be published within the year so that book reviewers can plan ahead of time to apportion their attention among books more equitably.

In addition to this haphazard dumping of books, another publishing practice that irritates booksellers is the habit of issuing books that virtually duplicate in their subject matter the books of competitive houses. Nothing succeeds like success, of course, and when one publisher scores a hit with a volume on flying saucers, or barbecue cookery, or with a pictorial history of the Civil War, it is only human for other publishers to want to get in on the act. Nevertheless, the practice of duplicating subjects even to the point of using almost identical titles frequently drives the bookseller wild, confuses the customer and is economically unsound.

Another point: it may be that publishers in their continual search for cheaper methods of production may one day decide, in line with the recommendations of various observers, to follow the French custom of issuing trade books *first* in paper editions and reserving the hard covers for those titles that have already proved themselves successful saleswise. This European procedure, which is exactly the reverse of our practice, might well deserve a try. But if we are unwilling to scrape away the barnacles from our thinking and save money, we might at least try eliminating the fancy jackets we now dress our books in (especially those titles with a 2,500-copy sales potential) and see whether this will affect sales adversely. I suspect not.

Whatever means will finally be used to modernize this industry and to bring it into the twentieth century, where every other segment of American business now operates, the time of reckoning is certainly at hand. Underpaid writers are not going to eschew indefinitely the more lucrative occupations of selling cosmetics, laying linoleum and driving laundry trucks in favor of tightening their belts and turning out esoteric studies on Boccaccio. Booksellers in ever increasing numbers will take out liquor licenses and consign Thomas Craven's volumes on art to hell; book editors will seek nice secure berths as advertising copy-writers, and finicky young patrons of literature, the Simons and Schusters, the Alfred Knopfs and Stanley Rineharts of the future, will put their money into the meat-packing industry unless publishing awakens from its torpor and shows some signs of returning a decent profit on their investment.

On second thought, why kid ourselves? Book people are not primarily interested in dollars and cents. If they weren't suffering from a satyriasis for literature, they would have entered occupations where real money can be made. For, strange as it seems, there *do* exist in this acquisitive society lovers of books who lust after non-pecuniary rewards with an appetite that causes them to stand out from the rest of men like a sore thumb on a Turkish masseur.

CHAPTER VII

Brass Rings for Gold

Human fallibility and frustration engender in man a necessity to believe in miracles. "If God didn't exist," Voltaire said, "men would find it necessary to invent him." Even the beautiful dream of Communism, the millennium when all men would be equal whether born so or not, couldn't replace in Russia the innate yearning for the supernatural; Stalin had to reopen the churches and let God return to the steppes.

A major industry ever since Alexander the Great promised the Greeks the whole world if they would just take Persia first has been the exploitation of human gullibility. Tricksters have proved time and again that the most outrageous lie will be believed by segments of the public—and in some cases by whole nations. Frauds have been perpetrated in every sphere of human endeavor.

The writing game has had almost more racketeers than the race track. Lord Byron was perhaps facetious when he charged that Barabbas, the insurrectionist who became immortal when he was released by Pilate in place of Christ, had been formerly a publisher. Byron need not be taken seriously; he would have garrotted his mother for a witticism, and the efforts of his publishers made him a fortune.

In Byron's day the sharpies and harpies of literature hadn't set up shop; the masses weren't literate enough to be fleeced. But now, with the mushrooming of state and private universities, junior colleges, mail-order courses in everything under the sun and other handy devices for becoming semi-educated, the American public has the notion that it is as easy to write literature as to propagate children.

A number of "literary agencies" have sprung up to accommodate the deluge.

As I stumbled along the misty-eyed road of publishing, I spent every waking moment, one way or another, in studying the business. I have told some of my discoveries, and made suggestions arising from the ideas they gave me, but it was constantly and abundantly borne in on me that the illegitimate side of the business could not be ignored; in fact, it had to be investigated thoroughly, for only out of inside knowledge could it be checked. No business can exist permanently half legal and half crooked.

This book is not an "exposé" and I am astride no white horse, but it is my conviction that publishers owe writers, who are the foundation of their business, more protection than they are getting. The Authors' League is a sectional institution that does excellent work; the very mention of its eminent legal staff sends cold shivers up the illegitimate operators' spines. But it seems to me that publishers as a whole ought not to depend solely on the Authors' League legal roustabouts when it comes to cleaning the literary house.

We have seen how crooks in the subsidy business brought discredit on all co-operative publishers. After determining my attitude toward them, I began to take an attitude toward other literary sharks.

Of these the fake literary agency may be the worst. (Note that I say "fake" literary agency. It is an important distinction, because all owe much to the excellent and reputable agencies which give genuine help to promising authors.) Just as publishers pretend to ignore the abuses in their own function, the genuine agencies seem to be content to work in their luxurious offices in studied ignorance of the crooked fringe which has appropriated their title. They could get together and in one way or another drive the crooks out of business, making life as difficult for them as the American Medical Association has made life difficult for the quacks. But they do not even have an effective organization with which to lobby, propagandize or improve publishing as a whole. They are like gamblers in Nevada, afraid to work together lest some among them may benefit. And so the reputable among them, like the honest among the gamblers, suffer for the sins of the few.

Make no mistake about it, the "literary" crooks are real criminals, of the sort that might be picking the pockets of the widow at the cemetery gates if more money were not to be made in fleecing amateur authors.

I found a good deal about these artists and the way they work. Rosemary Glotz has just completed her first novel. Whether it's a real novel or not is beside the question: she thinks it is. But how to get it published? In a newspaper she comes across an advertisement:

> If you can read this, you can write! Perhaps you have a manuscript of powerful originality that needs just a little polishing to make it salable. We would *love* to see it!

For a small fee, the advertisement continues, the agency will within ten days send a detailed criticism: "Our critic will point out your mistakes, your crudities and your assets." Rosemary learns that among famous alumni of this great agency are Lafcadio Smooch (who now writes regularly for the *Saturday Evening Post*), Rubiro Porticoso, the Brazilian novelist, and the celebrated novelist Alma Smiles. "We have marketed the work of thousands of unknown writers—why not let us do the same for you!"

Rosemary Glotz is impressed and also perhaps a little chagrined at her own ignorance; she has never heard of Alma or Rubiro. She is not unintelligent, merely ignorant of the devious maze she enters. She reasons that the agency must deal in good material; otherwise they would not be able to sell to publishers. So she parcels her manuscript, which she has had typed on rag bond at a cost of around a hundred dollars, and sends it in.

A week later Rosemary receives a letter signed by the head of the agency, a Mr. Oswald Puncture, who informs her that the novel has been received and is being given a preliminary reading to determine its possibilities.

A few days pass and then our Miss Glotz is made jubilant. Her manuscript, a second letter informs her, has passed the initial reading and is considered salable. But—and "but" is an important word in the lexicon of the literary crooks—while it is salable, it is not *publishable*—not as it stands. It needs some rephrasing and polishing and its construction wants tightening. If Rosemary would like expert help in this, the letter continues, the agency will be pleased to do the work for her. *But* the agency, alas, has to consider the matter of overhead; editors must be paid; still, since the agency is convinced of the ultimate worth of the novel, it will take a chance and offer Rosemary a specially low price. If she will send twenty-five dollars . . .

This plausible appeal seems reasonable to Rosemary, who milks her savings account of twenty-five dollars and sends it in. She is now on the hook.

A week later Rosemary receives a third letter, informing her that the work on the manuscript is being carried forward on schedule and would she please remit an additional fifty dollars to cover the cost? Rosemary is flabbergasted. She had assumed that the initial twenty-five dollars had taken care of this labor; and she writes a letter to Mr. Puncture asking him to clarify the situation. He replies that the twenty-five dollars had simply been a retaining fee to reserve the editor's time, whereas the fifty dollars covers the cost of the actual labor (at fifty cents per thousand words as stated explicitly in the national advertisements).

Rosemary sends the money. She decides that the error must have been hers. She had misunderstood the advertisements. Since her story has gone so far, she will not ruin its chances at this point.

In due course, the analysis arrives. It is a lengthy letter, an impressive dissertation on the technique of writing, with pointers on style, structure, characterization and tricks of exposition. The letter picks her manuscript to pieces, points out where the narrative missed fire, how the dramatic situation broke down, where the language is trite.

Mr. Puncture concludes, "Your basic story *is interesting* and *powerful*. It has freshness and originality. Do you, my dear Miss Glotz, realize how fortunate you are, how rare a thing is originality? *Anybody* can learn technique. But the important thing is what one *feels*. It is obvious from your writing that you have suffered and yearned and known what life is. It so happens that for authors in your predicament we have established a Revision Service in which we will undertake a thorough revision of your manuscript, eliminate all structural weaknesses, make the novel salable. When this has been done, we will assume complete responsibility for sending your story to the best publishers. We tailor your book to meet the needs of the current market. *There is absolutely no charge for our marketing service.* The cost of the Revision Service varies with the length of manuscript, and in the case of your novel, it will be $250, a modest fee for the services rendered. Only after your story is sold will we deduct our 10 per cent commission for marketing it."

Two months later, the revised manuscript is returned to her for her "approval." She rushes up to her room and with palpitating heart begins to read the revised copy that will bring her fame. Her heart sinks after the first ten pages. The story doesn't seem to be any improvement over the original at all. It doesn't keep her glued to her seat till the final page. It doesn't read like something by Daphne du Maurier or Frances Parkinson Keyes. It still seems to read very much like Rosemary Glotz.

Depressed and with definite misgivings, she sends it back to the agency and requests that it be marketed as soon as possible. Over the next five months she writes letter after letter asking for news. Eventually she receives a reply. It is a brief note listing an impressive number of publishers to whom the manuscript has been submitted and enclosing a rejection slip from each.

Rosemary writes the agency an indignant letter accusing it of taking $325 from her fraudulently. She receives a brief, dignified reply from Mr. Puncture, who regrets that Miss Glotz has been laboring under a misapprehension. If Miss Glotz will read the advertisements carefully, she will see that the agency does *not* guarantee publication of a manuscript. It is paid merely to revise and edit material, "not to contribute essential literary quality." The agency has submitted the manuscript to the leading publishers and they have found it unsuitable. "You accepted our Revision Service *voluntarily* and we are amazed that you now make charges of bad faith on our part. Since you are unappreciative of our efforts, we are returning the manuscript immediately under separate cover."

Mr. Oswald Puncture has been doing very nicely, thank you, with elderly retired lecturers, broken-down schoolmarms, zealous crackpots and other message-bearers in a class with poor Rosemary Glotz. The fleecing is accomplished with the efficiency of a salami slicer. Mr. Puncture's "editorial experts" are scissors-and-paste hacks who earn subway money doing piecework for him. The real labor is done by a battery of typists.

All communications are form letters, sent out according to a coded system. Even the "personal criticism" is actually nothing but generalized double talk. Mr. Puncture's typists sometimes make embarrassing mistakes. A client will receive for his detailed critical analysis the identical form letter he was mailed for his preliminary reading report. He will hit the ceiling and threaten to sue for fraud. But usually he is mollified by a quick refund of his money. Mr. Puncture's sole qualification for his role as literary agent is his skill at turning out letters seductive enough to part a sucker from his money, yet sufficiently foolproof to withstand any action in a court of law.

It should be said again that there are legitimate literary agencies that bear no resemblance to the characters described above. But the amateur writer would do well to investigate the standing of any agency that tries to lure him with a play to his "unheralded" genius.

How to tell a genuine agent from a fraud? Well, it's perhaps unwise to generalize and there are some notable exceptions, but I would say that any agent who asks a reading fee is automatically suspect. The top-notch agents, of whom there are perhaps a hundred in the country, mostly in New York, ask of the author only a fee of 10 per cent of his royalties. Since there aren't any royalties unless the book is published, it follows that to exist these agents have to be pretty good salesmen.

There are plenty of good reasons why even the most successful author should have an agent. For the beginning author he is even more important, for many publishers and editors and *all* motion-picture companies will refuse to read a manuscript unless it is submitted by an agent. In making this rule editors and publishers help to protect themselves against plagiarism. They know the agent, they don't know you. It was formerly quite a widely spread practice for a "writer" with no more literary equipment than a typewriter to sit down and copy, or perchance translate, stories and articles published a long while ago or in a foreign country, making, perhaps, slight changes as to period and locale. These he would submit to a publisher or magazine under his own name as author. Sometimes he was caught—editors' memories are long—more often he was not discovered until the story had been published and the check long since cashed. By that time the "author" would have changed his address and be assiduously copying somebody else's story under a different alias. Agents in general are not taken in because they are in closer contact with the writer and most agents won't take any writer on unless they have assured themselves of his bona fides.

Moreover, the agents perform another important function; their offices provide a first screening of a literary product. An agent is naturally not going to waste his time or money on a manuscript unless he thinks it has a chance to sell. Manuscripts sent in by the good agents have a much better chance of being immediately accepted than those that arrive, as the saying is, "over the transom."

Whenever one of my authors shows signs of being a success, I counsel him strongly to get a good agent to guide him along the way. The agent will take 10 per cent of his royalties, but he earns his money by the services he renders, including his knowledge of money to be made in subsidiary rights—serial, dramatic, motion picture and foreign translation.

No author can know all the editors and publishers but the agent, if he's really good, does. From long experience he can tell from reading a script, or from his reader's report (all the good agents have staffs of readers), where it has the best chance to sell. He knows the markets of the moment and the idiosyncrasies of editors and publishers.

Occasionally enterprising agents perform a real service by ferreting out foreign writers of promise or exotic reputation and having their work translated for submission to the American market. One of the top New York agents, a woman, "discovered" in this way a Scandinavian novelist who already was famous in his own country. She had one of his novels translated and sent it around; it was accepted, published and became a national best-seller. That agent deserved the very large sums she made. The author's best market ever since has been the United States and he threatens to come here to live.

The agent is on the receiving end of even more zany ideas for books than an editor. One literary aspirant—an acrobat—informed an agent I know that he planned to walk across the United States on his hands. He estimated it would take him ten years to proceed from Maine to California, and that there would be an exciting travel book in the venture. "If you can get a publishing advance to cover my expenses, I'll start out immediately."

Of course, in describing the workings of Mr. Puncture, I feel a little like Sisyphus rolling a rock uphill. Amateur writers will continue to patronize racketeers. The truth is that most people want to be fooled, to be taken in by the peddlers of poppy illusions. They want to be hoodwinked by a song and dance. For even after the final penny has been taken and a man has been turned out into the alley, the melody lingers on in his ears.

Not only have ham writers been hoaxed about the salability of their output; readers, too, have been deluded about the nature of their reading material. It may come as a shock to some who are accustomed to treating the printed word with respect to learn that the history of literature is also, in part, of course, the story of literary plagiarisms. There has been no limit to the exploitation of human credulity.

Christopher Marlowe stole whole passages from Spenser's *Faerie Queene* for his play; Sir Walter Scott printed in his own name a volume of poems sent to him by another; Edward Bulwer-Lytton plagiarized from George Sand; Thomas Hardy pilfered an entire chapter for a novel from an obscure American writer. James Whitcomb Riley, when he began to write, forged Poe's name to one of his apprentice poems to gain critical attention. (The critics applauded it as a literary masterpiece.)

The same situation applies in art. Wealthy connoisseurs have been separated from large sums of money through their gullibility. Eight thousand paintings have been sold in the United States and England as authentic Corots, although the artist didn't paint a third that number. Van Dyck completed seventy-odd canvases, but at least two thousand art lovers have signed "Van Dycks" on their walls. Twenty years ago three art collectors paid $300,000 each for Da Vinci's *Mona Lisa,* which had been stolen from the Louvre. (Each thought he had obtained the original; all three were copies.)

In the 1920's Alceo Dossena, an impoverished Italian

sculptor who was unable to sell work in his own name, "dug up" fragments of statues which he claimed were ruins from the Renaissance. These "remains" were judged by the world's foremost art experts to be the works of Michelangelo and his colleagues, and they were purchased by the Metropolitan, the Cleveland and Berlin art museums. For ten years the sculptor continued to "dig up" one valuable piece after another, selling his "discoveries" for millions of dollars. When he finally confessed that he had sculptured the work and buried it himself, he turned many an expert's face a blushing scarlet.

People in other fields who should have known better have been fooled. John Ruskin, the critic, once called a letter to which Thomas Carlyle's name had been forged "one of the most significant utterances of the master."

When Fritz Kreisler, a beginner, found it difficult to get a hearing for his compositions, he passed them off as the music of early masters, Vivaldi, Monteverdi, Boccherini, disclosing that he had "discovered" them during his world travels, and music critics wrote enthusiastic analyses of these "masterpieces."

Knowing the penchant of silent-movie producers for exotic talent, Theda Bara, America's first screen vamp, fooled Hollywood moguls by posing as an Arabian princess to obtain her first roles. She was the daughter of a Cincinnati storekeeper.

Two editors of a Cornell student newspaper, to confirm a theory that men in public life were not less gullible than the next fellow, formed an organization "to rescue from oblivion" one Hugo N. Frye, "the father of the Republican party in the State of New York." They sent invitations to high-ranking politicians to attend a dinner commemorating Frye's birthday. Enthusiastic replies were received from the Vice-President of the United States, the Chairman of the Republican National Committee and leading Republican congressmen. The Secretary of Labor wrote, "It is a pleasure to testify to the career of that sturdy patriot who first planted the ideals of our party in this region of the country."

The following day, the hoax was revealed. The celebrated Hugo N. Frye existed only in the minds of the students as a variation of the homely phrase, "You go and fry!"

Alexander Kahn, a celebrated Parisian impresario, got a kick out of planting fakes in American newspapers with the connivance of a famous correspondent. The "ghost of Mascagni" had conducted a performance at the Paris Opera, confounding psychical experts. When Maeterlinck's scandalous liaison with Georgette LeBlanc sent Maeterlinck (and Georgette) into the seclusion of a Seine château, Kahn sent word that the poet was actually en route to America. Even in those pre-tabloid days scandal was scandal and reporters covered every ship arriving in New York. Ten days passed and then a tip sent newsmen to a hotel in Boston; Maeterlinck had arrived there secretly and was sequestered in a private suite. For days reporters camped in the corridor before a locked door, guarded whenever food trays were sent up by house detectives. At the end of a week with excitement at its zenith the door was flung open and the newspapermen surged in to be received by a bearded "Maeterlinck," who gave them a statement in a voice with a thick Belgian accent. The statement said the poet was "through" with Georgette forever.

In the course of hours the interview was republished in Paris papers, copies of which reached the real Maeterlinck and his Georgette in their château, and Georgette was so angry that Maeterlinck had to consent to a photograph taken of them both. When reporters returned to the Boston hotel the private suite was empty, the Harvard student who had posed as Maeterlinck had decamped, beard and all.

Once a Swedish travel writer mentioned a South Sea

island he had come across that had been "unexplored" by white men for centuries. He drew diagrams of its location and provoked the Swedish Government into outfitting an expedition to visit the island and claim it for the fatherland. After the expedition had sailed for weeks without sighting it, the writer explained to enraged officials that he hadn't actually stated the island existed *but merely showed where it could be found if it did exist.*

Time and again we can return to the files of literature to discover how the shrewdest people have been fooled. One morning a Frenchman, Louis de Rougemont, walked into the editorial offices of a leading British magazine and claimed that he had undergone an experience unique in the annals of white men. He declared that he had spent thirty years as chief of a tribe of Australian cannibals. He was bombarded with questions by anthropologists, sociologists and geographers intimately acquainted with the Australian bush country. They certified his story as absolutely authentic.

According to Rougemont, he had gone on a pearl-fishing expedition in the South Seas. On the way home the fleet had run into a typhoon and had been wrecked. Rougemont managed to swim to a sandbar, where he lived for a time like Robinson Crusoe. Finally he built a boat and reached the Australian mainland, debarking among cannibals. He owed his life, he explained, to the fact that they looked upon him as a deity. After living among them for several years, they asked him to become their chief. He accepted and mounted his hair on strips of whalebone two feet high, and painted his face in four colors signifying the highest rank. He had two children by a native woman. Only the whiteness of their hands betrayed that they were half-breed. By a simple ruse he put a stop to the continual warfare between his tribe and its neighbors. In his very first battle, he mounted stilts seven feet high and marched at the head of his army looking like a giant god in war paint. The enemy broke ranks and fled in terror. Thereafter his people enjoyed peace.

For thirty years Rougemont ruled as chief, keeping up his guise as a deity by performing constant miracles. He collected charcoal, sulphur and saltpeter and made gunpowder, astonishing the natives with the explosion. He found a deposit of crude petroleum and delighted them with the weird "witch flames" he produced. Eventually he grew tired of the life. Seized with a longing for civilization, he made his way out of the bush country, fell in with a party of gold prospectors (the first white men he had met in over a generation) and made his way gradually to England.

The British magazine editors snapped up Rougemont's story and published it as a serial amid a fanfare of publicity. It caused an international sensation. Editors from Spain to Sweden cabled for permission to reproduce it. Top London hostesses vied with one another to obtain Rougemont for their parties. Vast crowds mobbed him as he walked along the street. The French Government crowed, "Who said a Frenchman is incapable of ruling over backward peoples!" The celebrated artist John Tussaud painted Rougemont and exhibited the portrait in a leading gallery. Rougemont lectured before the British Association for the Advancement of Science. It was freely declared by scientists that his contributions to anthropology and sociology would revolutionize these studies.

And then suddenly the storm broke. A picture of Rougemont had been wired to Australia and reproduced in a leading newspaper. The following morning a woman rushed into the editor's office and waved the paper in his face. "What lies are you printing about this man? His name isn't Louis de Rougemont. It's Henri Louis Grin."

The editor's jaw dropped. "How do you know?"

"I'm his wife. This man has deserted me."

Alas, the bubble burst; the glorious reign of De Rougemont was at an end. Louis, far from being a cannibal chief, had been an obscure butler and all-round handy man to a family of tradespeople in Australia. He had been no nearer the bush country than the author of this book. But Henri Louis Grin had a sparkling imagination and a world of gall.

To escape the wrath of the British public, Henri fled to the Continent. He was last heard from in India, where he appeared as a music-hall entertainer, billing himself as "The Greatest Liar on Earth."

With people as ingenious as Henri walking the earth, the life of an editor is strewn with booby traps. To this day, every time a publisher issues an autobiography, he crosses his fingers hoping that his author will not turn out to be another Rougemont.

And this has happened. Two fairly recent disciples of the Australian bunco man were Trader Horn and Joan Lowell of *Cradle in the Deep*. Trader Horn's autobiography was a literary sensation under the inspired merchandising of Simon and Schuster. Billed as the greatest true adventure story ever told, it was finally exposed as fiction. "I think," wrote one critic who helped in the exposure, "if Trader Horn had the Ogowe River dished up to him on a plate, he would not have recognized it."

Simon and Schuster had been taken in like everybody else; but, convinced that lightning could not strike twice, they subsequently put out Joan Lowell's autobiography in which the author recounted how she had stowed away as a tot on her father's ship in the South Seas, how she had been reared on the milk of a Norfolk goat, had jumped into the ocean to capture a sea horse for a toy and had learned about sex by dissecting a masculine shark.

Significantly enough, the disclosure that *Trader Horn* and *Cradle in the Deep* were phonies didn't hurt their sale one iota. A charming faker is far more acceptable than an honest frump. The people who had handed over their money under the impression they were buying the truth remained to cheer the fiction. After all, Joan Lowell was not a whit less sexy for being posed for pictures against fake backgrounds; and if Trader Horn had not actually met Stanley or rescued Cecil Rhodes from a crocodile, the story was a mighty exciting one anyway.

As a matter of fact, the reverence people have for the printed word is amazing. Simply because a man appears in print, the public assumes that he has something authoritative to say. This applies on every level. All of us have seen semi-literates reading the sports page of a newspaper on a street-car. They form each word reverently with their lips as though they were committing a litany to memory. The lower one's sophistication, the more he lavishes love on newsprint. Indeed, the reverence for the *written* word can be as acute among the intelligentsia as worship for print is chronic among low-brows. Brains do not always protect a man from playing an ass.

Two centuries ago, William Ireland, an eighteen-year-old bookseller, wrote a drama in mediocre blank verse and claimed that it was a lost play of Shakespeare that he had discovered among the heirlooms of his ancestor (who, he alleged, had been friendly with Shakespeare's family). Dr. Samuel Johnson, James Boswell, Richard Brinsley Sheridan and other leading critics went into ecstasy over the "find." Covent Garden and Drury Lane competed with the honor of presenting the "masterpiece." For a period of ten years, as fast as he could dash one off, Ireland turned up one piddling piece after another in the name of the bard, and he had all England by the ears.

Eventually William's conscience bothered him and he confessed the fraud. But not before he had added a cycle of historical dramas from William the Conqueror to Queen Elizabeth to the Shakespearean repertory.

Buncoana is a fascinating study and it is, of course, the life and soul of advertising. You will often hear that people don't believe in advertising any more. They never did. You do not have to believe to buy. Look into your own home and see how many possessions were bought—consciously or unconsciously—because of persistent advertising. Advertising today is the science of reiteration.

How does publishing stand in relation to the twin handmaidens of prosperity, advertising and publicity? It was important to me that I find this out, and I think I owe you my conclusions.

CHAPTER VIII

Wanted: A Gray Flannel Suit

If I'm a cynic (and I don't think I am), then cynicism is the acceptance of fact. However, you can't sell fact unless you dress it up in dreams, and in the twentieth century dream-peddling has been raised to an honored profession. It is the basic ingredient of salesmanship, the power behind the merchandising of maidenform bras, popcorn and God.

Am I a cynic because I think that in the field of books (between the covers of which the feats of history's great bunco men have been preserved) the possibilities of salesmanship, developed to a high point in other fields, are in the main ignored?

The book industry needs a Barnum. More than anything else we need master publicists with a genius for turning literature into front-page news. Men like Harry Reichenbach, who took hold of the movie industry when it was floundering as a five-cent attraction and boosted it into one of the major industries. We could use the talents of the obscure publicist who dignified the humble soda cracker by calling it a "biscuit" and thereby making "Uneeda Biscuit" an eleventh American commandment. The ugliest sow's ear can be turned into a silken purse by a first-class and imaginative public-relations man.

Harry Reichenbach was the most inspired manufacturer of hot air this side of Hades: he turned hoodwinking into a fine art and built an empire on the single assumption that any man can be sold anything if only you know how to do it. Back in 1912 movies were the laugh of show business; people walked out on them as they closed the vaudeville show. Established actors would rather have been found dead than caught in a movie under their own names. This situation changed somewhat when the greatest actress of all time, Sarah Bernhardt, appeared in a picture, but the industry still hadn't moved out of the Fourteenth Street nickelodeons operated by Adolf Zuckor when Reichenbach joined a newly formed corporation, Metro.

Metro had been stalling exhibitors for a year, promising to produce a picture. But it had neither the actors nor the money, and the trade was beginning to think it would fold before a camera began to crank.

The president called in Reichenbach. "Harry, how many pages can you write saying nothing?"

"I guess I can do about thirty pages."

"Splendid. Do it."

To cover thirty pages for the trade, Harry began with the discovery of America. As he later recalled it, he described Queen Isabella's pearls, King Ferdinand's beard and Columbus' passion for eggs. Then he told about the French and Indian Wars, the first railroad trains, and traced the progress of the nation up to the founding of Metro. At the end of each page he added the mystifying question, "Can They Keep It Up?"

The movie exhibitors asked, "Keep *what* up?"

"Just wait and see," Reichenbach answered with a dreamy look. He had a flag raised on Times Square and petitioned the City Council to change it to Metro Square. Still Metro hadn't produced a picture. But everybody marveled and asked one another, "Can They Keep It Up?"

Something decisive had to be done. Reichenbach went to the International Exposition in Los Angeles and actually talked the judges into presenting Metro pictures with a gold medal "for making the most important contribution to motion pictures for the year." They still hadn't put out a single film, but the news of the award was impressive, and the exhibitors were satisfied that Metro was keeping it up. The slogan tided the corporation over a period of financial reorganization. Finally it quit its stalling, signed Ethel Barrymore and Francis X. Bushman to contracts and laid the foundation of the present MGM Corporation.

It is interesting to note that on the single occasion Reichenbach devoted his talents to promoting a book, he turned it from a dud into a sensational best-seller. This was *Three Weeks* by Elinor Glyn. Harry arranged for post offices all over the country to be bombarded by letters from anti-vice societies, parent and teacher organizations, calling attention to the asterisks at the end of a love scene. By taking a dull book and ballyhooing it as forbidden fruit, he racked up one of the biggest sales records in history. There is no telling what miracles could have taken place in bookselling if the industry had developed its own Harry Reichenbachs to devote their careers to it.

The basic formula for a best-seller is either standard mediocrity or the delusion created by an illusion. This, I might add, is the formula for big business in America. If not, I defy anybody traveling in a strange town to venture into an untested restaurant when there is a Howard Johnson handy.

The fact of the matter is that publishing has no masters of ballyhoo. It has no tradition of dynamic publicity. It hasn't developed even a basic, standard procedure for advertising its merchandise. Most publishers will concede that they do not know how to advertise their books effectively. They point out that no two books present exactly the same problem and that a successful advertising plan for one will not necessarily be a good one for another. When a cigar manufacturer finds out by experiment how to advertise his cigars, his problem is solved. The advertisement of a cigar today will help sell the brand next year. The manufacturer gets cumulative effect from his advertising. But the novel that is advertised today will usually be dead within six months. There is no cumulative effect to be obtained in book advertising.

It should be pointed out, however, that movie moguls, like book publishers, face exactly the same problem of selling a new product each time out. No two pictures are alike. I believe that the publicity methods of Harry Reichenbach, Russell Birdwell and other topflight movie publicists have shown how to sell creative merchandise. What publishers need is a little of the ingenuity displayed by Hollywood promoters. Then they would cease harping on their problems.

Here and there in the book industry, it must be conceded, there have been businesslike attempts to cash in on human credulity. The Simon and Schuster people, Doubleday, the Book-of-the-Month Club promoters, have laid the foundation for an effective psychological warfare aimed at exploiting this gullibility on a mass scale. The previously mentioned success Simon and Schuster enjoyed with *Trader Horn, Cradle in the Deep,* and the exploitation of Durant's *Story of Philosophy* are cases in point. They were the result of an astute merchandising philosophy.

The Simon and Schuster, Book-of-the-Month people have developed a subtle flank attack to wear down buying resistance. They have become specialists in "culture publishing." (Several psychologists have analyzed the technique.)

The key word in this publishing formula is "panic"—the publishers "panic" the public into buying a book. They build around a title an atmosphere of cultural exclusiveness. "The smart, the sophisticated, the people in the 'know,' the delightful hostess, the much-sought-after guest—everybody who is in the swim of things—has bought a copy of the *Outline of Bunk.*" Week after week the tomtoms of publicity continue to pound, whipping up a tribal spirit into a deafening crescendo. Week after week the mounting sales figures are emblazoned across the country. The reader who has not yet bought a copy fidgets in his seat; he feels himself an intellectual pariah. Finally, disregarding the last appeal of his common sense, he rushes out to the nearest bookstore and pays four dollars for the book. It was with such a technique that S. and S. lured Ziegfeld chorus girls into reading Durant and Viking made call girls literate with *Ask Me Another.*

The Book-of-the-Month Club adopted this technique of psychological warfare with notable success. Every month six hundred thousand people sit down to read simultaneously the latest "literary discovery" of the judges who announce that they are offering a "great book worthy of national attention." Every thirty days the mob switches in its huzzahs from one title to another.

Of course, the theory on which the club operates is absurd. Anybody with a grain of common sense should know that books qualifying as "great literary discoveries" are not produced every thirty days with machine-like regularity. Furthermore, if an intelligent man is able to make a dozen books a permanent part of him during his lifetime, he is getting the utmost out of literature. But the merchandising ingenuity of the Book-of-the-Month panics the mob into devouring books quickly and restlessly, makes the reader feel anxious lest he be caught *flagrante delicto* with an outmoded book (two months behindtimes) in his hands.

As psychologists have observed, it is easy enough to recognize a panic. To create one is the hallmark of the greatly gifted. So long as Harry Scherman of Book-of-the-Month, Messrs. Simon and Schuster, and Ken McCormick of Doubleday are around to lend their inspiration, there is hope that the industry as a whole will not remain a wallflower unwooed by Mammon.

Most publishers, however, are loath to face up to the realities of their role in a democracy, and to adopt publicity weapons suitable to the situation, because they cling wistfully to the tradition that pictures them as professional descendants of the Elizabethan aristocracy to whom the promotion of literature was a sport, not a means of earning a living. Although the industry in fact has been thoroughly penetrated by commercialism, many publishers still feel compelled to keep up the myth of their chastity, to pretend to virginity when all the world knows that they have been forced to sleep around to pay their rent.

American publishing has stumbled upon curious and perplexing times. Today a man who has a combination of relatively mediocre qualities and wears a neatly pressed suit can make a million dollars as a master of ceremonies on television. The socially idolized American is the fellow who has mastered the art of talking and saying nothing. Balzac once declared that Paris was a city where great ideas were done to death by a witticism. It might be said that New York is the modern headquarters of a culture where ideas are strangled by a wisecrack.

William H. Gilbert once epitomized the dilemma in which a democracy finds itself by observing, "When everyone is somebody, then no one's *anybody.*" Most individuals yearn to develop "personality," to achieve exclusiveness, to be regarded as someone apart from the masses. Yet in our culture-for-the-millions atmosphere these very concepts are being reduced to an absurdity. When syndicated columnists offer to divulge to millions of readers the secret of acquiring a magnetic personality, the concept of personality no longer means anything. When a manufacturer who sells millions of bottles of whisky declares that he is catering to "the man of distinction," the term becomes meaningless. When a seaside resort with four thousand rooms advertises that it gives "the individual touch," the word "individual" has become ridiculous.

Whether this is a good or an evil society to live in depends upon one's point of view. A bull is a rather ugly-looking animal; but he looks mighty inviting to a cow. For better or worse, we are living in an era in which traditional values are decomposing and dynamic new forces have broken loose from a Pandora's box—forces which have yet to be clothed in suitable concepts and whose direction has yet to be charted.

Under pressure of present-day demands, and caught in the tension of the times, publishers react equivocally. They seem to be driven by a split personality, behaving part of the time as though they were in a profession, part of the time as though they were carrying on a business, acting snobbish and demagogic by turns, behaving as though they wished and yet didn't wish to belong to the twentieth century. In surrendering to commercialism yet at the same time decrying the mercenary spirit of television, movies and other forms of competitive entertainment, publishers behave like the circus woman who spends her days lying on the points of dozens of swords, yet rails at her husband for eating crackers in bed.

It seems to me that publishers must get down to brass tacks, face the facts squarely, adjust wholeheartedly body and soul to the role that has been thrust upon them—and play it with gusto wherever it leads them. I would suggest that the industry strive to attain the complete lack of self-consciousness of the movies and the circus; that it unashamedly encourage modern Barnums and Reichenbachs to play the piper's tunes that will lure millions to the box office.

This apparently is an age in which an individual has unlimited license to deceive others; but he is severely penalized if he is naïve enough to delude himself. Publishers should quit deluding themselves as to the nature of their present-day function. They are manufacturers of a product that can potentially serve every American who has mastered the intricacies of the alphabet. This being the case, they should make use of all the promotional tricks their ingenuity suggests to reach the millions. Why shouldn't a present-day Reichenbach be encouraged to dress up an orangoutang in evening clothes and turn him loose in Gopher Prairie to publicize a new edition of Darwin's *Origin of Species?* How about advertising a new issue of *Leaves of Grass* in electric lights to raise the eyebrows along Main Street? Mount Parnassus could certainly use a publicity genius who can hammer into the consciousness of the American people "Uneeda Book" with the same tenacity a press agent once merchandised the humble soda cracker.

Current publicity methods in the publishing business today are entirely inadequate. Instead of employing experts at getting book news into the press, flashing it over television, writing it across the skies, too many publishing houses employ sweet young things, fresh from a course in journalism at Vassar, who are adequate only for arranging literary teas and entertaining disgruntled authors and visiting delegations of schoolteachers and librarians. Publishers act as if book reading should be an exclusive hobby practiced by the eccentric fringes of society.

Ezra Pound once said, "Literature is news that stays news." There is no doubt in my own mind that any book worthy of being published at all is *news,* and that the writer who developed the book is *news,* and with the proper exploitation could find his way into the newspapers along with everything else that interests the American people. In my own firm I have had success promoting authors as news. Elsewhere I have outlined specific techniques I have found useful for this promotion; they can be employed by any publisher whose eye is on the ball.

America's culture is more personality-conscious than any other civilization has ever been. Give a person a "name" and he can live on it. The average reader accepts the gossip of columnists as contemporary folklore. That is what publicity agents have been selling; and both they and their clients—especially female personalities—have wolves whistling before their doors. For this reason, I was amazed to read Herman Wouk's plea of anonymity in the New York *Post* in his complaining postscript to a series of articles about him published by that newspaper. "A writer," he said, "is nothing but a gray dirt-covered root. The works he sends up into the sunlight are his fruits, and only those are worthy of attention. But when a writer is lucky enough to find an audience, he becomes a legitimate object of journalism. He cannot justly complain of the loss of privacy. Nobody asked him to seek public attention by writing books." All I can say is, such an attitude is not for the public—it's for the birds.

Publishers must learn to peddle dreams—and not for the destructive ends of the hoaxter but for the constructive purpose of making literature news. Let us excite people into craving what we have to offer. To be big business we have to think in terms of big business.

A new Harry Reichenbach could bring books into the American home, make them almost as popular as toothpaste or Luckies or television—if we could find him and give him concerted backing. Individual publishers, men with a flair for publicity like Dick Simon, have made a success with individual books. What the industry needs is to sell the book-reading *habit* to the American people. It could be, after all, less harmful than cigarettes.

Modern homes have built-in stoves, built-in beds, built-in baths, built-in ovens, built-in refrigerators, built-in everything—except built-in bookshelves. Three things make a house look like a home: a child's toy, a picture on the wall and books. Toys are merchandised by the million. Even pictures have made a reappearance on painted walls. But in thousands of American homes you won't find a single book. This is the age of the grandiloquent promise, of the Pied Piper. Maybe we ought to update children's literature so that nursery rhymes chant the slogan "Don't be a gook; own a book."

CHAPTER IX

"The Editor Regrets . . ."

In discussing the people who carry the ball for the book industry, I have reserved for this chapter observations on the T quarterback, the fellow who calls the plays on Saturday and frequently ends up astride a rail in a coat of tar and feathers donated by the Monday-morning quarterbacks.

The editor-in-chief has virtually the most thankless job in a publishing house. He buys his groceries and pays his rent on the basis of the good guesses he has made for his firm. The cemeteries are filled with the crosses of editors who turned down *David Harums, Vanity Fairs, East Lynnes* and *Outlines of History,* only to let rival firms turn them into record best-sellers. Actually, there is something a little "tetched" in the head about a man who devotes his career to trying to evaluate in dollars and cents the public response to a number of small, black, esoteric dots inked by authors on a sheet of paper.

It is not surprising that an editor's judgment is frequently fallible. Even the most able critics of an era have had curious blind spots in evaluating contemporary talent, either inflating it or deflating it to absurd lengths. A scribbler by the name of Bowles was praised for years as a poetic genius by both Shelley and Keats. He died before either of them and has never been heard about since except by students of literary curiosa. On the other hand, Voltaire thought that Shakespeare was a barbarian; Wordsworth damned *Candide* as tripe; Swinburne loathed Walt Whitman and called Tennyson a hack; Thackeray saw no talent whatever in Dickens: "He will never outlive his times." Dr. Johnson considered Fielding's *Tom Jones* a monstrosity; Coleridge called Thomas Gray a mediocrity.

One can't blame an editor for letting a big fish off the hook. Usually he is too busy throwing minnows back into the stream to notice the prizes that wriggle away. The editor of even a small-sized publishing house is deluged with so much bilge watered in human misery that if he hadn't jacked himself into a mood for punching an orphan in the teeth he would spend his days doing nothing but twisting a handkerchief.

One editor of my acquaintance recently received the following letter from a woman. (And it was by no means the low point in his experience.)

> DEAR SIR:
>
> I understand that you publish books. As I am very poor, I thought you might buy any novel I may decide to write. Please let me know as soon as possible how much you can pay for it. Could you furnish me with the paper to write the manuscript on and deduct the price of it when I deliver the book? Must I have a license to write manuscripts? How much would it cost? Should the story be written in good English or can you put it into shape for me? Without seeing the story can you give me an estimate of how much I can earn from it, providing you advertise it well?

Letters like this, which should properly be submitted to the department of human welfare or to the misery shows over television, find their way by the score into editorial offices.

The great time-consuming procedure of an editorial department is the winnowing of manuscripts. Many of the novels submitted have been written by lonely men and women who have been consciously or subconsciously imitating some recent big successes in fiction. Some fifty thousand manuscripts that a trade publisher can never be persuaded to invest his money in are making the rounds of publishing houses at all times. Some of them come back to the same reader four or five times, occasionally with a superficial face-lifting and a new title substituted to hoodwink the unwary.

A certain percentage of all manuscripts are marginal or borderline books, and these provide the editor with his severest test. Either he must gamble upon publishing an uncertainty or face the possibility of the new author being signed by another house which may be able to nurse him along in the space of three or more books into a big best-seller and valuable property.

Even today there are times—although the practice was more general before present high-level production costs—when a publisher, remembering the slow development of John Steinbeck, Sinclair Lewis, Joseph Hergesheimer or Willa Cather, will accept the book of a new writer not because it is a finished work in itself but because it seems to indicate promise of later fulfillment. Steinbeck and company to the contrary, statistics reveal that this kind of gamble rarely pans out. Nine times out of ten the second novel is no better than the first, and frequently it is worse. After two or three duds, the writer is dropped by the publisher and never heard from again.

Harrison Smith, literary lion of the *Saturday Review,* one of the most perceptive minds in publishing, once invited me to lunch when I had just hit my stride as a publisher by issuing over a hundred books that year, practically singlehanded. I was overawed by the invitation.

At luncheon he told me that a survey he had made revealed that publishers did not make a profit on novelists until their third or fourth book. With production costs and overhead mounting in geometric proportions, novelists were going a-begging, because publishers could not afford to nurse them along.

I revealed how I published novels for about $1,500, how, along with good publicity—even then I knew that advertising alone never sold literature—an author could stand a chance. However, we both agreed that the unwieldy departmentalization and conventional procedures more than doubled the cost and made this impractical for large publishing houses. And I left unsaid the fact that a best-selling author is the "favorite author," and that he gets the lion's share of time and effort—not to mention promotion budgets—which overshadow worthy but less commercially sure authors. Nor did I feel confident that the trade publisher would give a modest budget and a complete vote of confidence to an especially dedicated editorial task force to storm entrenched literary bastions.

One of the curiosities of our publishing world is the boom and bust of the one-shot novelist. When an influential publisher sends out a review copy of a novel written by his fair-haired "discovery," a number of reviewers will shamelessly dish up purple adjectives heralding the debut of a genius. None of these reviewers are simple-minded dupes; but a number of them, realizing that the publisher is looking for rave notices to use on his jacket, and not averse to getting their own name on a jacket for a free publicity ride, think nothing of writing exaggerated blurbs.

When reviews are not entirely favorable, publishers will edit them to elicit the necessary raves. For example, a critic will write: "I found Mr. Fairhead's style rather exciting, though the story itself was contrived. Certain situations were mildly provocative; but the total effect is something less than brilliant. The novel is basically a tour de force."

The blurb on the publisher's jacket will read: "Style . . . exciting; situations . . . provocative . . . brilliant . . . tour de force."

Too often the sequel to this abnormal booming is an ignominious crash. The number of one-shot novelists living in this country who are never heard from after a spectacular debut is amazing. The promise an editor may sense in a novice, his faith in the maturing of his abilities, has frequently been smashed by the operation of forces beyond the purlieus of the editorial sanctum. The editor's own perspicacity is not to be blamed.

Despite the influential role editors have played in the shaping of manuscripts celebrated in literature, they generally remain obscure fellows as far as the general public is concerned. Even the intelligent layman, outside of informed circles, if asked to name the great editors of the twentieth century would probably be stumped after mentioning Maxwell Perkins of Scribner's, the mentor of Wolfe, Hemingway, Fitzgerald and James Jones.

No outsider knows to what extent the great books of history owe their final form—indeed their very existence—to the contributions of editors who worked behind the scenes with the authors. The only recent case history publicized has revealed to what an extraordinary extent Perkins pruned, clarified and reshaped Thomas Wolfe's writing into communicable form.

It would be an intriguing undertaking for somebody to write a history of editorial responsibility for our literary classics. Unfortunately, the evidence is untraceable and the story can never be known. As the critic John T. Winterich once observed, "Readers give as much credit to an editor for the books they read as pitchers pay tribute to the horses whose hides encase baseballs." And, of course, authors have not shouted their gratitude from the housetops.

Like the psychoanalyst, the editor in most publishing houses deals with clients in various stages of maladjustment, suffering from emotional blocks, guilt complexes and hostility. He has to deal with the author who, having started out writing fiction for the pulps at a cent a word, has reached the point at which he is rewriting the same stuff for slicks and hard-cover books at ten times the money and who seethes with guilt and hatred toward the world for foisting this irony upon him.

Or take the spinster who appears with an autobiographical manuscript daintily tied with a ribbon which describes a heroine's wild ride to a tourist cabin, a few drinks, her sexual yielding and subsequent abandonment to her betrayer. What can an editor do with this "love letter" submitted to him? Return it with regrets and stay clear of the author.

And then there is the shy bald-headed little fellow with horn-rimmed glasses and a baby-pink complexion who under various female pseudonyms turns out a weekly story for the women's confession magazines. (He is the most successful writer in the field.) And there is the burned-out, penniless roué who was thrown out of every bar on Broadway until he struck gold writing bunny-rabbit stories for preschool children and made enough money to keep him on a champagne drunk for a lifetime.

In addition, the editor must deal with the 300-pound

author who ambles like a baboon and turns out exquisite little rondeaus and other filigree lyrics in the spirit of Emily Dickinson; and the writer who is always under contract to do books the publisher thought of and urged him to write—who paces the sanctum pleading with the editor, "Will you let me go off on an intellectual binge just once and write *my* kind of book!"

There is no question that writers, especially the successful ones, have their idiosyncrasies that plague the life of even the most understanding occupant of the inner sanctum.

It is a matter of record that some writers have used unconventional means to prod themselves into creative achievement. They have been known to sit with their feet in a steaming bath or on a cake of ice, or to inhale the odor of fermented fruit as they wait, pencil in hand, to catch an inspiration. One novelist of no mean achievement could write only with a mandrake poultice on his head. Gertrude Atherton once retired to a room on the summit of a mountain and wrote furiously for fifty days while a snowstorm raged about her rattling the walls and windows. The moment the storm stopped, her inspiration ceased. Elinor Glyn wrote in bed with her head turned to the north. Booth Tarkington once went to southern Italy to begin a novel, but when the sunshine failed to spur his inspiration, he returned home and retired into his bathroom, where he wrote the entire book. Goethe confessed that he found the greatest inspiration for composition during sexual intercourse. He would try out the rhythms of his hexameters by tapping them on the buttocks of his partner.

It is certainly not easy for an editor to play nursemaid to writers. But his troubles are not limited to these. An editor is continually under pressure to pass judgment on writing according to standards that would cause a fastidious literary critic to wince. Once upon a time, as has already been indicated, writing was looked upon as a glorious sport that was never meant to be debased by money. As a matter of fact, this attitude lingered for centuries among devotees of literature, even after some of them went into the publishing end for a livelihood. In the 1880's American publishers competed with one another for the consumer's dollar in the fraternal spirit of Harvard oarsmen meeting Yale for the traditional race up the Thames. It was all so truly sporting. (As this is written, book salesmen are referred to by the trade as "travelers," a euphemism which dates back to the days when a chorus girl's legs were referred to as "limbs.")

When editors began to practice, Americans were not harassed by the pace of modern living. Leisurely editors inscribed letters to their authors in a special copying ink; each page was inserted between leaves of tissue paper which, after being wet with a brush and pressed in a vise, retained the duplicate of the original. Manuscripts were indeed manuscripts in those days, written laboriously in pen and ink. When an editor wanted to speak to an author in a hurry, he cranked a grotesque contraption at his elbow with all the vigor of a later-day consumer cranking up his model-T Ford.

In those idyllic times the literary agent had not yet made his appearance and publishers were not high-pressured into bidding vigorously for authors at fancy prices. Editors were not titillated by MGM or Twentieth Century–Fox money to select manuscripts for book publication that could be turned pronto into scripts for the movie millions. Editors were not lured by the financial cooings of book clubs into bartering mush. They could afford to gamble on their own enthusiasms, to okay novels that might not reach a sale of one thousand copies, but which would warm the hearts of a discerning few.

Today, of course, an editor's judgment is circumscribed to an unprecedented degree by the shadow cast by Uncle Sam's lettuce. The reasons for an editor's selection of a manuscript are various, but all of them usually boil down to questions of expediency. "This manuscript isn't any great shakes," he considers, "but I understand that the author's last book sold twenty thousand copies." . . . "Three of the top booksellers on the Pacific Coast sent us rave letters about the author's previous book and they promise to put this one over big because they sold hundreds of his previous book." Or "The author is a close friend of a critic who has been giving us some good breaks." Or again, "There is another publisher who is going to put out a book on this subject and I'm sure we can beat him to it."

The very most a conscientious editor can undertake to do is to present books of the best quality that people can be persuaded to accept—and let it go at that. Unfortunately, the amount of time people now are willing to give to reading at any level is shockingly small. A recent survey indicates that Americans devote twelve times as many hours to thumbing through magazines, watching television and going to movies as to reading books.

Like all thoughtful people, the editor is baffled by the question, "What happens to the millions of Americans who were made into book readers when they went to school? What happens to their reading habits the moment they get a high school or college diploma in their hands?" But the goal of an editor is more modest than the winning of millions back to books. He would be content if, through his selections, he could steadily increase the number of titles reaching sales of ten and twenty-five thousand copies annually.

The editor lives in a society that has reached the highest

level of material comfort in history. Judged by previous standards, things are relatively comfortable for the American professional writer. Even if he can't sell his manuscripts, his wife earns good money writing copy for an advertising agency. The people around him are well fed, too. The writer has no genuine incentive to write masterpieces as Tolstoy did about the starving peasantry. "How are we going to write the Russian masterpiece in America," wails one critic, "as long as life here goes on so *unterribly*?"

Those writers who have reached the top live like merchant princes, entirely bonded to the ideology of big business. Erskine Caldwell poses as a Man of Distinction for a Calvert Whisky ad; Hemingway displays his hirsute charm in the service of a fountain-pen manufacturer; another top-flight writer publicly quaffs a nationally advertised beer. Even when an author gathers material about okies, sharecroppers or Negro millhands for a social novel, his purpose is usually not to launch a crusade but to climb aboard the best-seller lists. The American proletarian novel is a book about the poor designed to be read by the well-to-do.

On top of this frankly commercial spirit with which the modern author pursues the editor and brings additional pressure to bear upon whatever aesthetic integrity he might possess, there is the further complication that the traditional guideposts of criticism no longer can be applied to much that is turned out by a number of contemporary writers. In an age in which departments of knowledge are so overspecialized that faculty members usually talk with one another only about the rainfall and the weaknesses of the faculty administration, a number of nonconformist artists have paradoxically broken from the limits of their own bailiwicks and wandered promiscuously into their neighbors' stamping grounds. Today some composers tell stories, novelists preach sermons, painters philosophize and poets lapse into everything but verse. The harried book editor is in some instances hard put to decide whether he is called upon to pass judgment on flesh, fowl or good red herring.

Nine times out of ten, he will seek refuge behind the conventional mush that pours into his office by the bagful—manuscripts that at least are intelligible, if not very intelligent; that reassure him by their unswerving devotion to the obvious. Picking his way past the snares that are laid for him by unorthodox contributors, the editor can safely fall back upon basic types of entrées. Slick costume fiction interlarded with sex is usually likely to pay off the costs of publication. Autobiographies continue to be a profitable genre of nonfiction. They may be written by the famous or the infamous; the chief qualification is that the author has enjoyed experiences denied to most of us and that his reputation warrants the expense of a good ghost writer. Another branch of writing that editors can depend on is the solidly written biography. Travel and adventure books also have their following. Expert technical books are in demand; and sometimes an alert editor will ferret out a layman who, in the exercise of a hobby, has acquired specialized knowledge that can be turned, with editorial guidance, into a profitable book.

The field is as wide as social interests and as deep as human misery. Thus, for example, I developed a sixteen-page baking-school manual into a book that sold, and is selling well, as *Decorating Cakes for Fun and Profit.*

And, when an advertising man shoved a much rejected manuscript called *How to Stop Snoring* under my nose, I knew it had possibilities. Snoring has given America more sleepless nights than national election returns, and I remembered that snoring has not only been the cause of divorce, attempted murder, but even got a G.I. an honorable discharge from the army during the heat of World War II. I decided to snap it up. I kept the produced book under wraps until I discovered a two-line item in the Chicago *Tribune* about a pending divorce, in which the harassed wife could not tolerate her snoring spouse. A long-distance call, two bottles of bourbon and an air-mailed book got me a front-page story, with picture, in which even the judge felt that this book could save the marriage. The story broke world-wide wire services, and the book went into four editions.

One type of book that calls for a highly specialized form of editing is the subscription volume. Frequently subscription publications are reference works for family use and they are sold house to house in sets. While the series may be put together under the direction of an outside educator, the house editor must co-operate very closely in its preparation. The standards of accuracy are particularly exacting and the editorial headaches can be numerous.

Subscription-book selling is older than the nation. As a young man George Washington went on the road selling from door to door. Daniel Webster was a book agent and so was Ulysses B. Grant just before the Civil War. Rutherford B. Hayes, another future President, was a book canvasser, and, of course, Parson Weems, in peddling his *Life of Washington*, became the most colorful book agent in history.

Editors who are specialists in preparing subscription volumes are highly prized by publishers, because subscription selling has always been one of the most lucrative branches of the industry. At various times the dollar volume in book canvassing has exceeded the dollar volume of books sold over the counter.

A leading subscription publisher tells how he once canvassed a backwoods area with a book on arithmetic. He called on a prospect and made the sale. But when he asked for the customer's signature on the order form, he had to call in a neighbor to witness the man's mark. It goes without saying that this prospect would never have gone into a bookstore to buy this volume. It was necessary for a salesman to seek him out.

Subscription selling operates on the principle that a number of people can be persuaded to buy books when they are *personally* convinced of their benefits. The same principle applies to selling life insurance. No one would walk into a department store to buy a policy over a counter, no matter how manifest were its benefits. Indeed, various insurance companies have engaged in test advertising of policies at unusual bargain rates for people who would come into the district office for them. The ads were flops. Insurance, like certain types of books, can be sold only when the agent goes into the home and clinches the order.

Subscription selling hit its stride at the end of the nineteenth century when thousands of Americans who had no intention of opening a book nevertheless desired to build a home library as a hallmark of social standing. Numerous sets of Dickens, Thackeray and Scott were sold by subscription; many an adult today made his initial acquaintance with these writers because the books stared down at him from his father's bookshelf.

Subscription selling is still growing, and the editor of a subscription house usually has a lifetime job if he desires it. Subscription books, along with textbooks, constitute the most stable publishing item today.

But let us leave the secure rear echelons and return to

the man operating in the ulcer belt. I have friends who have become successful trade editors whose preparation for the emotional upheaval in which they operate was by no means conventional. Many editors were gifted neurotics even before they had the whammy of a business title put on them. Some editors were practicing authors before they pledged themselves to earn a dollar a little more frequently by putting on a tie and collar and going to work. I knew one high-brow editor with a Harvard accent and a homburg who formerly toiled for the pulps and who even now, between spells of shoulder rubbing with the literary smart set, turns out spicy detective stories.

Another editor high up in the literary bluebook also started out as a writer. He wanted desperately to carry on in the tradition of Kafka. But the great novel wouldn't come. He sweated and drank and tumbled the wives of his neighbors; but he still couldn't squeeze out a line of genius. The upshot was that he decided to quit trying to write a masterpiece and became an editor instead. He joined a publishing firm and sat in judgment on other people's brainchildren.

The best among the good many book editors I know had to be born to the job. They must know not only what the writer should say but how to get him to say it. Publishers have lost authors because of maladroit handling by editors who tried to inject too much of their own personality with too little regard for that of the author. A creative writer if he is any good has a strongly developed personality and he is likely to have a very different background from the editor's.

The author of several best-sellers approached one of the largest New York publishing houses with the idea of writing an historical novel based on the shipment of women to Tasmania a century ago. Tasmania had been a dumping ground for convicts. The British Government had given them their freedom, land, seeds, tools and credit for food—everything but the one thing the convicts hadn't seen for years but wanted more than men had ever wanted anything in the history of the world: women.

Some of them hadn't seen a woman for ten years, none for less than five, except for the few wives of army officers who, when they went shopping in Hobart, went guarded by a corporal's squad. They petitioned the home government to send women.

Back at home there was a surplus of women, and when the government advertised for young, strong, capable women to emigrate to a colony where jobs at high wages were guaranteed there was an instant response. The applicants knew, of course, that they would find not only jobs in Tasmania but husbands also, and living as they did in a land where there were two women for every man, this appealed to them as a way to end the drabness of their lonely lives. The government sent out a number of these so-called "girl ships," including not only regular applicants who had paid their twenty-five-dollar passage but also the sweepings of the female jails.

Our author's book concerned one such ship, based throughout on historical record. His unfortunate characters—fictional, of course—went through every misfortune imaginable in their odyssey to the promised land. The ship suffered plague, fire, tempests and famine. There was also a mutiny when some of the crew tried to seize the ship to sell the women as slaves in Brazil. This failed, but when the ship reached the Derwent heads, two days from Hobart up the Derwent River, she was six months out of Plymouth and more than half of her passengers were dead.

The other half, sailing at last up the placid Derwent,

looked with tired but yearning eyes on the misty, heather-cloaked land which resembled Scotland. This was the promised land.

They did not know what was happening in Hobart. The ship had been signaled from the Derwent Cape; five thousand woman-crazed ex-convicts had come to town and for forty-eight hours had been drinking the town dry in celebration of the approaching revels.

When the ship docked the women were mobbed by a lust-mad army of drunken, fighting men. Historical records showed that half of the women who landed were raped to death. Of those who survived, many were crippled for life.

There was no need, the author thought, to embellish the facts or to drag them out. They were so horrible that they couldn't be exaggerated. So he wrote the scene as history, exactly as it occurred.

Soon after he received a note from the woman editor whom the publisher had appointed to work with him on the book. "More sex in the rape scene, please," she wrote. The note so enraged our author that he threw the product of eighteen months' research and work out of the window and refused to finish the book.

Whatever his or her background, there is no doubt that an editor today operates in an area as large as life with all its nuances of laughter and tragedy. Sometimes he holds not only reputations and destinies in his hands, but life as well.

At the Cock & Bull in Hollywood I was told one afternoon of a very sensitive author who had written several delightful novels and who in consequence—it was the early days of sound—had been hired by one of the big studios as a writer. He was given one of his own books to script and spent six months on it, producing an adaptation into which had gone his best and finest thoughts. He sent it to the studio, the studio sent it to a producer and the producer gave it to a reader. Three weeks later the author was found with a bullet in his brain, the script beside him. Scrawled across the script in blue pencil was the succinct criticism by the reader of his cherished work. It was in one word: "Stinks!"

Well might O. Henry say that the two saddest phrases in English language are "please remit payment" and *"the editor regrets . . ."*

CHAPTER X

The Inner Sanctum

So the great day has come. Your book has been accepted for publication. You gather your wife or your girl in your arms and you say, "Come on, kid, let's celebrate." You go out, you get beautifully lit and you go home to bed to dream of huge royalties with which you will buy a yacht and cruise around the world.

Brother, I wish I could join you. You have, at any rate, got over the first hurdle. There are a few more ahead (a *few!*), but you'll get over them too, in time. Only, as your publisher, I would say better wait awhile before pricing that yacht. But acceptance is the big hurdle. Numbers of manuscripts are returned for reasons that have nothing to do with their merit.

The editor may already have accepted a book on the same subject; or the reader may have had too terrible a hang-over the morning your manuscript arrived, and been unable to appreciate your jolly sense of humor. Or the book may have pleased the editor, but he felt that it wouldn't be commercially successful. When an editor has had a quarrel with his wife, even a manuscript by Kathleen Norris on marital bliss might well be rejected by him. If his boy has just failed to be graduated from high school, a manuscript on juvenile delinquency becomes a personal issue. The Lord knows how much first-rate reading the public has been deprived of through the years because an editor at the mercy of "house policy" shoved it into the "outgoing" basket.

Many a manuscript fails to achieve publication by a hair's breadth, which often accounts for the history of repeated rejections of many famous and successful books.

Hard-pressed writers, competing with a spate of rival petitioners for an editor's approval, will turn verbal somersaults to attract the editorial eye. One editor I know received the following note enclosed with the author's manuscript. "Read my novel and then decide which of us is a lunatic—you or I."

A poet sent to an editor of a sophisticated magazine the following verse enclosed with his poem:

> Please, gentle soul, if you are able
> Accept my poem—yes, please do.
> If you refuse, I'll blow a fuse,
> For my apartment rent is due.

The editor wrote back: "Which poem have you submitted for consideration? The piece about your rent being due is by far the better of the two. Perplexedly yours . . ."

A woman wrote the editor of a romance magazine: "Here is your big opportunity to accept a *real* love story. If you are the man I think you are after seeing your picture printed recently, I am sure you will have the courage to cut loose from the usual drivel you publish and use the strong meat I am enclosing." The editor glanced through a couple of paragraphs of high thermal content and wrote back hastily, "That picture you saw *flattered* me!"

It is, of course, no secret that authors—notoriously thin-skinned fellows, for all their ability at character assassination—rarely attend the funeral of an editor. (They enthusiastically endorse the burial, of course, but cannot spare the tears to be present.) The only question in many a writer's mind is whether an editor was born a scoundrel or whether he got that way on the job. An author's bitterness is frequently unassuaged even after he comes into fame and fortune. True enough, the bile may be occasionally sweetened by a chuckle.

Ralph Henry Barbour, the writer of boys' stories some years back, once published for the beginning author instructions on how to make an editor's life even more miserable than it is. Since editors prefer manuscripts to be typed on a uniform-size paper 8½ by 11 inches, Barbour recommended that the tyro use paper half that size and write diagonally in pen across the narrow portion of the page. Once the manuscript is completed, the writer should take care that his pages are *not* numbered consecutively. "Personally I misplace them by tens." As a means of impressing one's personality upon an editor, Barbour fondly cites the example of a novice who enclosed a cleverly designed cylinder bomb in the roll of his manuscript. "He had the right idea; but unfortunately the mechanism failed to work on time and the explosion did not take place until the office boy was rewrapping the manuscript for return."

Humor aside, there is certainly room for improvement of relations between authors and editors if the book industry is to become a more prosperous one. After all, the interests of both author and editor are the same. One cannot exist without the other.

Another cross the editor bears is that his judgments regarding future sales performance of a manuscript are vitiated by certain destructive practices of the industry. For one thing the editor is under continual pressure to put together lists of new books every few months. No sooner has a plethora of books been crammed down the maw of the bookseller than these are looked upon by the publisher as outdated. The entire promotional efforts of the industry (with the exception of the reprinters) is geared to pushing *new* books. Publishers are obsessed with the notion that the *newness* of a book is a major incentive in the psychology of the buyer. There are indications that large numbers of Americans do not know whether the book they buy is six months or two years old and furthermore do not care. Certainly children are not generally concerned whether a favorite book of theirs was published yesterday or fifty years ago. Nothing "dates" with them. However, in their mad rush to replace one book with another, publishers have been cutting their own throats.

Each of the titles on a publisher's list is not only in competition with the titles of a rival firm, but in competition with its catalogue companions. Getting one out of fifty books published into the average bookstore, and seeing to it that at least one book in a hundred is properly displayed, is a major problem. In competing for bookstore space, for advertising and publicity lineage, books on the same list are in the position of a hungry snake swallowing its own tail.

The life of a book under present conditions is tragically brief. Yet the editor adds new books to the stocks of the bookseller (who is having enough trouble selling what has already been dumped upon his counter). Furthermore, this indiscriminate spawning of trade books leeches into a publisher's backlist, usually the most profitable part of his business. Years of solid editorial labors which went into the building of a successful backlist can be virtually nullified by the editor's feverish adding of new titles under orders from his publisher.

The *Bookseller,* commenting on the 19,962 titles published in the United Kingdom in 1955, viewed with dismay the unrestricted publication of new titles, because more books are being issued than the public can assimilate. The result is the same in the United States. The only ones who benefit are the "remainder" buyers and bookstores, who rub their hands in gleeful anticipation at the profusion of books that are their guarantee of staying in business. Millions of books sold in this country are a deficit to their publishers, a loss of income to their authors and a 49-cent bargain to the reading public.

In our country, with its number and variety of inhabitants, it should be theoretically possible for any author of a worthwhile manuscript to find a loyal, if modest, public. Under a decent system of distribution this goal would be achieved. Today any meritorious book that fails to achieve a sale sufficient to break even is definitely the victim of individual publishing incompetence or of the ruinous practices of an industry that permits more products to be manufactured in competition with each other than in any business.

Instead of continuing to hunt obsessively for the elusive smash hit that leaves the industry as a whole no richer than before, editors should be encouraged to select books that will raise the general sales level of book buying. Today the percentage of Americans who are graduated from college is greater than the percentage that was graduated from high school a century ago. It is to be hoped that some day the editor will be free to select his manuscripts with some recognition of this educational development.

Actually, no book should be published to which a publisher is unable to give his complete and proper merchandising attention—in fairness to the author and to himself. In another section I have discussed the methods by which I have succeeded in publicizing my authors when thumbs were pointed down. In co-operation with my writers I have exploited every last ounce of business out of their home localities; and I have used this as a foundation for developing a wider interest.

Because of the nature of my business, I have become a

specialist in obtaining the utmost out of the book with the small sales potential, to the benefit of the author as well as myself. It is the trade publisher's credo to jackpot one book out of fifty into the fifty-thousand-seller class, instead of methodically raising the sales level of books from 5,000 copies to a level of 10,000 copies, and so forth up the scale. This is the only sound way that the market can be expanded. It cannot be overemphasized that increasing the sales of the total of "little" books, and not the freakish achievement of the occasional best-seller, will be the only genuine index of the industry's expansion.

One of the chief reasons trade publishing has not achieved the stability of other industries is simply because it is "best-seller" crazy. One cannot pick up a trade journal or read book advertising in the newspapers without continually coming across the term "best-seller." The label is flexible enough to cover a sale of five thousand or five hundred thousand copies; but the implications are misleading. The truth is that very, very few books over the years—either naughty or nice—have been genuine best-sellers. Furthermore, books claimed by interested parties to be leading the pack may not be the books that are selling best at all. The best-seller lists compiled by the New York *Times* and *Herald Tribune* have been found to be unreliable. They not only do not indicate the comparative sales between titles sold in the bookstores and titles sold through other media, but frequently they do not even give an accurate picture of the comparative sale of bookstore titles.

Surveys of the methods used to pick best-sellers (e.g., Cheney's *Economic Survey of the Book Industry,* Link and Hopf's *People and Books*) have revealed definite malpractices. A bookseller, asked to report on his sales, will notice out of the corner of his eye a pile of books he devoutly wishes would disappear from the counter. He has other titles on which he is heavily overstocked because of a publisher's high-pressure salesmanship. The bookseller will report these titles as his leading sellers.

In some instances a bookseller has been known to say to a publisher, "I'll promote your book if you will give me special co-operative advertising on it." Or, perhaps, the deal will involve a special discount. Any measure is employed to decrease the pile of unsold copies on the counter. The bookseller justifies his action by reasoning that if he and two hundred other retailers boom a book as a "best-seller" for several weeks, it may genuinely become one—especially if the publisher promotes it vigorously with special discounts and co-operative advertising.

Publishers rarely make public their actual sales. A completely distorted picture is frequently presented to the public. In any event, the best-seller label is used so indiscriminately as to be virtually meaningless.

Time and again I have had authors come to me after having a manuscript rejected by a trade publisher. They will boast that their previous book had been a "best-seller" (i.e., it had sold ten thousand copies). They usually exaggerate the sale by five thousand copies or more; however, accepting their claim at its face value, I reply, "In other words, there are still about 160,000,000 Americans who have never heard of you. Since you are known to only 1/160 of one per cent of the public we are going to have quite a job building you up!"

The conflicting claims of best-sellerism among competing houses would be hilarious if they weren't so tragic. As Cheney reported, publishing is the only important American business that knows virtually nothing about itself on a collective basis. Genuine statistics are as scarce as hens' teeth. Instead of attempting to clear the air with realistic statistics, publishers continue to send up smokescreens to lower the ceiling of visibility with extravagant claims and counterclaims.

By inflating his hand with poker-bluffing, a publisher often aborts the healthy demand for other books on his list that not only cannot compete with the speculative buildup given some books, but cannot survive it. Time and again, when a book has been boomed as a "best-seller," the crash has come so suddenly that booksellers are left overstocked with a worthless commodity. The publisher has deluded the bookseller, the public and, what is absolutely inexcusable from his own standpoint, himself!

In the meantime, when all is said and done, publishing is carrying on, if not always with the utmost wisdom, at least with an integrity and open-mindedness that give promise of better things. And the editor, despite his fetishes and perplexities, remains publishing's indispensable man. Even in this mechanistic age, the educated guess, the inspired prophecy, continues to be enshrined in publishing tradition.

Recently, a celebrated psychologist, hearing publishers voice their traditional complaint about the speculative nature of their enterprise, suggested that they hire a corps of well-trained psychologists to make an exhaustive study of the books the public wants and then get them written to order by experts. In this way they could narrow the risk of publishing to a minimum.

"Why," the psychologist wanted to know, "do you fellows waste so much time on speculative experiments?"

One of the publishers present replied, "If we followed your method, what would happen? At the very best we would publish one commonplace book after another with only fair success. And then some little printer around the corner would print a novel that really stirred his heart. And the book would turn out to be a masterpiece. The little printer would become overnight a publisher with a great new author on his hands. And the publisher who adopted your methods would have descended to the level of a printer. No, there is no formula for salting the tail of genius."

So long as the majority of publishers still feel in their vitals this way, the editor is certain to survive.

CHAPTER XI

The Tilted Fig Leaf

When Upton Sinclair's *Brass Check* was banned in Boston because of the horizontal parallels drawn between Yellow Journalism and Red Lights, the issue was based on a single printed page in the book. After a time, he outmaneuvered them and for Boston consumption had a large fig leaf imprinted over the offending page.

I suspect that the lurid pictures on the covers of paperbacks, which seem to sell even the tamest books, are a development from the practice of booksellers who used to display many a "lurid book" by opening it to the shocking page and putting it in the shop window. Apparently the paper-back boys, whether they realized it or not, merely pictorialized the incident and updated it with Technicolor.

Whether this is a legitimate practice—or even a moral one—has been much debated lately. But an even longer-lived debate, still no closer to solution, concerns the validity of any censorship at all and to what extent the morals of minors and the feeble-minded can be "protected." I don't know how many remember a little book that had a great vogue in the thirties. It was called *Mother Goose Censored* and simply repeated the familiar rhymes with one word blacked out, thus:

Solomon Grundy
—— on Monday,
—— on Tuesday,

—— on Wednesday,
—— on Thursday,
—— on Friday,
—— on Saturday.

In a foreword, the editors suggested that the reader replace the dashes with a made-up word, like "oomph." And beneath the Grundy poem was a single line of italic comment: *Some man, Grundy.*

As a satire this little lampoon of the blue-pencil boys is nearly perfect. Censorship has been one of the banes of authors and publishers since the days of Cato, and perhaps earlier. A major chapter on the history of human stupidity could be written on the attempts of individuals and groups to define what is a good or an evil book and to enforce their dicta at the point of law. The book publisher has been sued time and again and has sometimes gone to jail in Star Chamber proceedings resulting from this madness.

In the enlightened year of 1955—and I quote from *Publishers' Weekly*—"The prize for the most ridiculous censoring of the year goes to Jackson, Mississippi, which early in the year passed a wildly sweeping ordinance making it illegal to sell a book which 'features any . . . act or conduct which has been condemned as a crime by the state of Mississippi.' Subsequently, three retailers were fined for selling copies of an . . . Earl Stanley Gardner mystery."

Heywood Broun once wrote that it was unfortunate that Anthony Comstock had not been present during the first week of creation; for the plan of sex might have been effectively suppressed by him at that time. But without the benefit of Comstock's penetrating wisdom, the Creator decided to divide the race into male and female and decreed that Comstock himself must be begotten in copulation

"Sex," to coin a paraphrase, "is a tragedy to him who feels and a comedy to him who thinks." But to the bluenose who neither thinks nor feels but only smells, it is a stinking thing—as stinking as his own dank mind, whose pose of prudery frequently conceals an advanced case of lechery wrapped in an anxiety complex.

Through the centuries the censor has put his dirty mark not only on writing but on all the creative arts. Indeed, one Italian censor, shocked by the undraped angels in Michelangelo's "Last Judgment," ordered a subsequent artist to cover their nakedness with loincloths. Postcards reproducing famous nudes in the Louvre have been confiscated by American customs authorities. When the Spanish Government, commemorating Goya, issued a postage stamp reproducing his most famous nude, "The Dutchess of Alba," the Watch and Ward Society in New England came across a stamp that had been mailed to America and deplored the fact that it was powerless to prevent its circulation.

Unfortunately, the mentality of the censor hasn't been confined only to the obviously unintelligent. During a production of Gilbert and Sullivan's *Pinafore* played by children, Lewis Carroll was shocked by the famous recitative in which the word "damme" appears several times. "I cannot find words to convey . . . the pain I felt in seeing those dear children taught to utter such words to amuse ears grown callous to their ghastly meaning." So remarked the author of *Alice in Wonderland,* a book that millions of people are under the impression was written by a man with a sense of humor.

Authors who have one time or another come under the censor's blue pencil read like a Who's Who of literary genius—Aristophanes, Ovid, Petronius, Rabelais, Boccaccio, Defoe, Sterne, Rousseau, Harris, Joyce. These and other writers have titillated obscure glands in the censor that apparently are not activated in the normal make-up. It is true that much great literature is flavored with erotica. But erotica, and for that matter pornography (which is a far different thing), have never yet been demonstrated to have driven a reader to commit a sex crime. A critic once wrote: "Books are written to be read by those who can understand them: their possible effect on those who cannot is a matter of medical rather than of literary interest."

Nowhere has literary censorship exposed its perverted psychology more dramatically than in Boston. Here, at the very time that Eugene O'Neill's *Strange Interlude* was banned from the stage, Ann Corio was allowed to strip in a burlesque house on Scollay Square. In fact, that celebrated burlesque house, the Old Howard, continued its bawdy contributions to Boston culture during the years in which Upton Sinclair, Theodore Dreiser and numbers of other writers were branded as immoral. The Boston situation signifies that the censors have never really been concerned with "filthiness" in literature, but with the unconventionality of certain authors who attack the religious, economic and political institutions that the Watch and Warders have appointed themselves to defend. But it is small comfort for the bookseller, often the scapegoat for censorship proceedings, to know that he is not actually being threatened with jail for distributing obscenity but for circulating progressive ideas.

All men are eccentric in varying degrees, and what is considered by the majority of "wise heads" in a community to be moral is merely a form of insanity that serves as a working adjustment to existing circumstances. "Nothing risqué, nothing gained," Channing Pollock told the American flappers in the twenties. And the flappers, with a recklessness born of desperation, tore loose from the flapdoodle philosophy of their elders, only to age into the conservative grandmothers of today's bohemian youth.

Although the bookseller has been put on the hot seat by the arbitrary judgments of censors, the movie exhibitor has been strait-jacketed by an even more rigid code of morals. It is in the pastures of Hollywood that censorship has really romped high, wide and handsome. The code devised by the amalgamated frumps has banned all kissing lasting for more than four feet of film. "Among acts or scenes that may not be shown are thumbing of the nose, slapping a woman's posterior, unmarried couples living together . . . a lover making an exit through the window . . . and the key to a young lady's apartment in the possession of a man not her husband." At one time even shots of naked infants were banned from the screen.

Once sex was effectively stifled on celluloid, the next step was to ban "politically subversive" themes. Morris Ernst in his book on censorship recalls how the United States and England once censored a Russian-made film portraying the Nazi persecution of Jews before the second World War. The censors feared that the picture would "inflame passions" against a nation with whom their countries were at peace. When the Soviets signed their non-aggression pact with Hitler in 1939, the film was precipitously banned in Russia and permitted entry into London and New York. The standards of political censorship shift with every gust of the wind.

Yes, censorship roams over a wide area, sometimes with unexpected results. On occasion the work of an author is enlisted for a cause he could not possibly have foreseen. When Hugh Antoine D'Arcy wrote *The Face on the Barroom Floor,* he certainly had no desire to curtail the pleasures of tippling. Indeed, he was a sworn devotee of the art. But the Anti-Saloon League got hold of his rollicking verse and distributed copies of it by the millions in a propaganda campaign for Prohibition. "If I had realized that my poem would help bring about the Eighteenth Amendment," muttered the poet in his cups, "I would have taken a flying leap into the Hudson River."

The average American is far more charitable toward sinners than the professional hair shirt. The women—and male masqueraders—who write for the "true confession" magazines about the transgressions of Mary Sue receive thousands of letters monthly from readers who offer the erring daughter or the debauched maiden aunt the use of their homes and other services of rehabilitation. "Tell Mary Sue to wire us that she will come and we will meet her at the station. We will take care of her like a daughter."

Even in Boston there are folk who have not lost their sense of proportion. When the Watch and Ward fraternity launched a drive to prohibit the teaching of sex in schools, one Beacon Hill scion was moved to set forth the dilemma of a family in verse:

"You are thirteen, my son," said the elegant dame,
"And of sex you're beginning to mutter.
There are facts you should know, but remember your name,
And learn in the *very best* gutter."

The American who without question devoured the most pornographic literature, thumbed the largest number of French postcards in our history, was Anthony Comstock, father of modern vice crusaders. Yet by Comstock's own testimony he remained uncorrupted to his final hour. This is in itself impressive evidence of the harmlessness of "filth."

The question of whether naughty literature can pervert a schoolgirl is a silly one. But there does remain a basic issue underlying the deceptive façade of the sexual question that is worth consideration. Immorality covers a much wider territory than mere sexuality. Problems that arise from it can be critical. Certain books *do* contain genuinely immoral themes; and the decision whether or not to disseminate them must be faced at some time or another by every publisher. He must decide whether a particular manuscript is calculated to add to the sum of the world's misery.

But what is an evil book? Was Machiavelli's *Prince* a factor in creating the cynical philosophy that spurred kings and statesmen to send armies across Europe, carve up their neighbors' territory and spill the blood of the masses for centuries? Was Nietzsche's cult of the superman partly responsible for the philosophy of Hitler? Is Marx's *Das Kapital* at fault for the religion of Communism which has created the present world crisis? Would the world be better off if *Mein Kampf* had never been published? What responsibility have publishers incurred for revolutions, wars, bigotry?

It is a matter of record that certain books have plumbed the emotions of large numbers of people. When Harriet Beecher Stowe, who wrote *Uncle Tom's Cabin,* was presented to Lincoln, the President inquired quite seriously, "Is this the little woman whose book started the big war?"

The public excitement stirred up by *Trilby* during its run as a magazine serial was tremendous. Just before the final installment, the editors received a letter from a woman who wrote that her sister, now on her deathbed, had expressed a wish to discover how the story ended before she died. The editors mailed the dying woman advance proofs of the last installment with the solicitude of Extreme Unction. Interest of people in Dickens was equally intense. When the British steamer brought the final installment of *The Old Curiosity Shop* into New York, a tremendous crowd gathered at the pier. "Is little Nell dead?" men and women called as the boat made port.

In certain cases writer and publisher function in socially influential roles, and they are duty-bound to take their responsibilities seriously. But what is a moral and what an immoral practice on the part of a writer? To mention a relatively minor instance—was it wrong for the agnostic Dr. Samuel Johnson, during periods of poverty, to write hack sermons pseudonymously and sell them to preachers at a guinea apiece to deliver in their Sunday pulpits? Was it wrong for Edgar Wallace, Sax Rohmer and others of their literary persuasion to mass-produce yellow journalism in book form?

In the case of Edgar Wallace, "mass production" is used advisedly. He was able to dictate a book a week. He prepared movie scenarios during weekends. Once when a play of his was being rehearsed in London, the producer wired him in New York that the last act needed repairs. Wallace got up early next morning, rewrote the last act—and the second one for good measure. He cabled them as a night letter; and the following morning they were in rehearsal.

The standard of good and evil in literature varies not only with the viewpoint of a censor but of an editor. George Jean Nathan, not one to subscribe to the Watch and Ward Society's standards of naughtiness, had his own standards of "obscenity" when he was editor of *Smart Set:*

> From stories in which the gay nocturnal life of the Latin Quarter is described by an author living in Dubuque, Iowa . . . from stories about . . . baseball players, cowboys . . . employees of the Hudson Bay Company, and great detectives . . . from stories in which the dissolute son of a department store owner tries to seduce a working girl in his father's employ and then goes on the water wagon and marries her as a tribute to her virtue . . . good Lord, deliver us!

These were the kind of stories Nathan placed on his private *index librorum prohibitorum.* They were guilty of the unpardonable crime of banality. Nathan's rule of thumb wasn't bigotry but discrimination.

Some insight into the mentality of the sex bigot can be gleaned from the fact that when he occasionally cuts loose from his moorings, he goes ribald in an epic way. One of the most erotic writers on record was formerly in holy orders. Another was an Anglican divine who went, unofficially, into spiritual exile. The first was Rabelais, the second Laurence Sterne. Only a renegade priest could have cut loose with such a grandiose display of lasciviousness as the French friar. And who but an English parson could have written *Tristram Shandy* and *A Sentimental Journey Through France and Italy* when he had finally severed his chains? Technically Sterne remained a minister preaching from the pulpit during his literary orgies. He was the phallic priest reincarnate, and nobody seemed to mind. (Of course, this was pre-Victorian England. It is obvious that neither Oscar Wilde nor Bernard Shaw ever had a chance of being invested in the Church of England.)

The question as to what is a good or evil book will never be answered definitively as long as men with varying philosophies inhabit the earth. Each publisher will have to wrestle with his own conscience as manuscripts are submitted to him. However, while it is impossible to characterize definitively as evil any particular example of writing, I believe that it certainly is feasible to label as evil a certain practice underlying the promotion of the type of books under discussion—and other literature as well.

Censorship is not an unmixed curse. It can be turned into a bonanza for a publisher. The banning of a book may create publicity that will transform the dullest story into a best-seller. Indeed, there have been instances in which publishers have deliberately issued censorable books and provoked an incident with the Watch and Ward Society to build sales.

The question of "naughtiness" in literature is regarded by publishers in terms not of morality but of salability. This is all very fine, except that it points up a situation which is financially, if not morally, unsound—the publisher's preoccupation with best-sellerism in general; his obsession for booming a title with any handy device, even censorship, at the expense of the industry as a whole.

Under present circumstances, the question of whether a book is good or evil is academic to a publisher or an author. The only question is, Will it hit the jackpot? Publishers have and will continue to publish books praising Joe McCarthy, attacking nonconforming government scientists, glorifying Polly Adler and Lucky Luciano, providing these will get a rise out of the buying public. Authors in a desperate scramble for big sales are trying their darndest in many instances to write material that will fall afoul of the censor's blue pencil, hoping to make a fortune out of their martyrdom.

However, a word of caution should be addressed to literary aspirants who hope to build a synthetic best-seller merely by scraping filth from the walls of the privy onto the printed page. No writer who has consciously "written down" to an audience—who has sprinkled his prose with the outhouse odors—has succeeded in permanently winning the masses. Readers are quick to spot a phony. In general, only the writer whose emotional sympathy is genuinely with the many and whose values coincide with theirs, whether they peddle hotcha or sweetness, can hope to write wide-selling books.

Fastidious authors who have tried to manufacture a potboiler have almost invariably failed. James Branch Cabell sells as a paper back imprint. Significantly, the only other time he enjoyed anything like a popular sale was the result of the Watch and Ward's banning of *Jurgen*. But relatively few people who purchased *Jurgen* as a result of the Watch and Ward's gratuitous advertising understood it.

What, then, is a good book—or a bad book? Breakfast is an occasion attended by all mankind. However, to the old New England Puritan it was a meal that launched a grim new day of psalm-singing. To a café society playboy it is the meal that ends the revels of the night before.

Speaking of censors, incidentally, reminds me by analogous reasoning that one of the hazards publishers encounter in piloting a book toward best-sellerdom is the literary critic, of whom I have spoken before. If the censor is the Scylla, he is also the Charybdis guarding the right of the passageway; and around him the publisher must cautiously thread his way if he isn't to be wrecked on the rocks. As in the case of censorship, an adverse book review can boomerang and bring a book large sales. A critic in San Francisco was so annoyed by the "filth" in a book (a best-seller and a Book-of-the-Month Club choice) that he wrote two columns denouncing it in the strongest terms he could use. It was a book about the Army in which practically all the characters were degenerates and the dialogue obscene. At a time when parents were seeing their boys inducted into the army to serve in Korea, the book was not only in bad taste, said the reviewer, it was so irresponsible as to be nearly criminal.

A few days after the review was published the reviewer received several hundred letters and telegrams of congratulations, the most fulsome of which was from the book's publisher, which said that since the review had appeared sales of the book in San Francisco had doubled.

This isn't always the case. A damning review can truly

damn, and often does; a publisher is never certain what the result of a review will be. Publishing is the only industry whose product, retailed in stores, is under the continuous fire of critics, in the very media financed by its own advertising money. There are critics—the major ones, particularly—who receive so many titles for review that they can't possibly find out whether the majority of the volumes are naughty or nice; and when they turn a title over to an assistant, his judgment is sometimes not worth the paper it is written on.

I have found in my own experience that books which frankly discuss sex, while they will usually not cause female reviewers to bat an eyelash, will move some masculine critics to blush to the roots of their pompadours. These spiritual transvestites who masquerade in pants will gag at books my aunt and yours would chuckle over.

Since it is healthy to keep a proper perspective, let us bear in mind that no matter how energetically the Watch and Ward Society waves the red flag and tips off the initiated that there is dynamite in a book, no matter how "sensationally" a title may take hold—it creates at best only a ripple of response from the Great American Public. About 499 out of 500 Americans who can read are never lured into buying a book, no matter how delightfully lascivious it may be.

So let the book censor, the critic and all those other gentlemen who get into a pother over the moral goings-on in the publishing world relax and take stock of their own surroundings. Not a single American woman would have been debauched an hour sooner than her time if James Joyce's *Ulysses* had been permitted to enter the United States legally a few years earlier. The young would not become juvenile delinquents in any greater numbers if the *Kama Sutra* were placed on the list of required high school reading. I doubt whether a scintilla of virtue would be added to the behavior of little boys and girls if Pollyanna today were mass-distributed in a comic strip.

I suspect that men loved and laid down their lives for their fellows long before they learned to read, and that lechery is beyond being corrupted any further by a book.

CHAPTER XII

The Royalty Road

Once writers were a class apart, distinguished by ink-stained fingers, unkempt hair and a predilection for drinking cheap wine in cellars. Mass education has changed all that; scratch any man on the street, and you will find a little printer's ink oozing out.

My business is about evenly divided between professional writers and nonprofessionals. In this last class are people from every walk of life, businessmen, industrialists, artisans, preachers, sailors, clerks, all of them with a story to tell but not needing to make money from writing to live. Some are extraordinarily successful and wealthy.

I have had many clients who have wanted their books published merely for their own amusement and for that of their family and friends. There is no great difference between a man ordering a yacht and a man ordering a book, and there is no reason why he shouldn't have either, if he can afford it. His book, though, will be a personal thing, because he will have authored it and long after the yacht has gone to the break-up yards the book will continue to give pride and pleasure.

Professional writers come to me for a variety of reasons. Sometimes they bring to me virgin typescripts of novels or nonfiction which they have written out of an inner compulsion, aware that their subjects are not commercial. Every year I publish books aimed at the motion-picture market—the studios pay four or five times more for printed and published material than they do for typewritten "originals."

In this connection there is the story of Darryl Zanuck, now production chief for Twentieth Century–Fox, who went to Warner Brothers just before the introduction of sound, said he was an author and asked for a job in the scenario department. To prove who he was Zanuck displayed a beautifully bound book—bearing a title and his name in large gilt letters as author. The scenario editor was suitably impressed and gave him a job, and within a year Zanuck had shown such genius in the work that Jack Warner made *him* scenario writer.

Only after he was firmly established did Zanuck show close cronies the book that had done the trick. It was a beautifully bound book, all right, but the four hundred pages inside were completely blank. Zanuck had had the job done himself at a local bindery. He had not written a line.

The movies have grown up since then and the studios are extremely selective about their material. It is a fact, though, that while the plot of a feature picture is generally that of a long novel—that is, a succession of incidents surrounding a small number of main characters—very few novels are easily adaptable for pictures, and often a "natural" picture plot would not have much success as a novel. Hence the novels we publish that are aimed more at producers in Hollywood than at the general public.

But the majority of professional writers come to me for publication because, although the trade has turned their scripts down, they have faith that if published the books will sell. And more often than you'd think they are right.

One of the reasons there are so many more professional writers today is the increasingly large number of schools and classes for writers, especially fiction. Some of these schools are popular departments of universities. Practically every university and college in the United States has a class in journalism, and about half have classes in general and fiction writing. A few of these last, notably those of Stanford, Yale, Harvard, Princeton and Chicago, have acquired deserved reputations through the successes of their alumni. From the west to the east coast are several writers' workshops, some operating as summer camps; one at least of these has a high professional standing and specializes in the writing of fiction and the drama.

Not all who want to write can go to universities or writers' workshops; a large army of hopefuls is scattered all over the land, most of them living in small towns where there is no one competent to teach writing as a trade. This situation has caused the emergence on the American cultural scene of dozens of correspondence schools for writers. Some of these are honest. Some are not.

Thousands of Americans receive instructions through the mail on how to plot a short story, develop character and situations that presumably will bring in money and adulation and perhaps a Pulitzer prize not long after the postman stops calling. The mail-order maestros wax exceedingly lyrical in their advertisements. They give the impression that, next to shooting a hot hand of crap, writing is the laziest way devised by man to make a fortune. Streams of success stories reveal that all a fellow requires is a pen and a ream of paper, and he needn't ever lift a finger to do an honest day's work again.

When the schools advertise there is a limitless demand for writers and when they reel off the names of scores of their graduates who are harvesting the fields of El Dorado, they are elaborating a lie. Book and magazine publishers are not panting for the literary effusions of Aunt Jennifer from Sioux City. Not one in hundreds of the men and women who pay the writing schools hard cash to liberate their muse will ever sell a word they write. The market isn't large enough to take care of all the professionals, let alone the amateurs. Only a half dozen of the slicks buy material at a decent price, and most of the output is supplied by a handful of established authors.

Recently, a survey conducted among professional writers disclosed that not a single one of the several hundred interviewed had received his training in a correspondence school. A number of distinguished authors whose pictures appear in the advertisements of the schools were found not to have been connected in any way with them. A subsequent survey, conducted exclusively among pulp-magazine hacks, revealed that a minority—less than one per cent—had taken a correspondence course in writing. The thousands of amateurs who annually receive mail-order diplomas simply enrich the dream merchants.

Occasionally, a beginning writer will run into grave danger. Lightning will strike—he will sell a story. Once he has seen himself in print, he is a "goner." On the strength of the few hundred dollars he has earned, he will give up his job, move his wife and family into humble quarters, sit down at the typewriter and strike out as a free-lance. The chances are that he will not sell another story for months, or even years, if at all. His ability to sell a story every thirty months or so does not mean that he has "arrived." Yet, having drawn blood, he will never abandon the illusion that he is a "pro."

The need to write is widely and deeply felt. Many people who never earn a dime at it write fiction for the same reason that others read it—as an escape from their routine, everyday lives.

Some use it even as an escape from prison. One of the largest writing schools in the country is in "The Little Gray

Home in the West," San Quentin. Students there have few of the ordinary worries besetting the writer. They pay no rent; their food and clothing and medical attention are free—and they have all the time in the world, or at least as much time as the judge has sentenced each one to "do."

They have found, these convict writers, that though their cells are locked and the high walls manned by guards with machine guns, they can escape from prison whenever they sit down to write—or to paint, for the prison has an art school too. Their muse can take them wherever they wish to go in the world outside from which their physical bodies are barred.

There have been numerous successes by San Quentin authors (some of the convicts, of course, were writers before they were admitted) and at least two books, one by a denizen of the death house, have caused sensations. The prisoners also publish and print their own newspaper and magazine, often of a high literary quality.

In one year no fewer than fourteen hundred prisoners submitted poems for publication. Nearly all were nostalgic in theme and a few darned good.

There is a tremendous amount of job snobbery in our society. The laborer, the white-collar clerk, even the executive, bogged down in the rut of earning a living, constantly seeks to escape from his routine existence. This fragmented living, which has become the hallmark of our times, is imposed on us from our schooldays. "Let us know how you wish to earn your living," say the educators in effect, "and we will eliminate from your education everything that does not lead directly to that goal." If the high-school graduate is going to be a business secretary, all she needs is a business education. To acquaint her with Renaissance painting, the philosophy of the ancient Greeks and other landmarks along the highway of human culture would be, according to modern values, a waste of time. To operate an I.B.M. machine, or drive a bus or punch a cash register, one need not have an appreciation of the spiritual forces that have placed man upright upon his two legs and inspired him to look to the stars.

Even our universities are vocational factories, supplying human tools for the assembly lines. When a market opens up for industrial psychologists, the universities enlarge their psychology departments, hire new instructors and produce industrial psychologists like robots to supply the demand. When a call goes out for petroleum chemists, the chemistry laboratories become overcrowded; reinforcements are trained and poured into industry.

There is a vocational need for virtually every type of man but the *whole* man. Our society specializes in fragments, fractions, digits. The factory worker, if he shows any pride at all in his job, boasts of his achievements in numbers. "Today I turned out six thousand bottlecaps on the assembly belt. Tomorrow I hope to step up my production to seven thousand."

It is no wonder that people, as a means of refuge, weave secret dreams in which the factory whistle, the crowded subway ride and the monthly bills are brushed into temporary oblivion. Writing—even poor writing—is an attempt by an individual to piece together the fragments of his personality into a coherent whole. All over America people dream themselves into the roles of authors. In fact, there have been cases of star-struck individuals who have gone so far as to impersonate the role publicly. Once, two impostors passed themselves off as Edna Ferber and Octavius Roy Cohen on the same lecture platform—and neither knew that the other was a phony.

One writer, a spirit medium who took a correspondence course, informed her instructors that she receives her plots from the great authors of the past with whom she communicated during seances. Under their guidance she wrote about places she had never seen, countries she didn't know existed and peoples who were utterly strange to her. Another lady submitted a manuscript I'm afraid we hadn't time to read, even though she assured us that the spirits had told her the book would sell a million copies—and would I kindly mail her a check for $50,000 advance royalties?

The maternal complex developed oddly in another woman, who wrote, or rather ghost-wrote, the autobiography of her small son from the moment of his first chortle to the day he joined the Cub Scouts.

Most of this output is uninspired. But consider its source. One critic, with more understanding of his fellows than certain others, observed, "So long as it is possible for a human being to be born and brought up under the Third Avenue el, it is useless deprecating his literary standards. We must begin by changing Third Avenue." Well, Third Avenue *is* being changed—but a new "Third Avenue" is arising somewhere else.

There is nothing wrong in encouraging people to write. In some cases it is useful therapy in the treatment of disordered lives. But anyone who holds out to the untalented writer the hope that he can make a living as a writer is a fraud. The correspondence schools commit this crime daily.

The life of even a popular writer isn't all champagne and flowers. Established authors, men of talent, sometimes have to wait years between the publication of manuscripts. Sometimes, on the strength of an early winner, a writer will buy a lavish house in Westchester; just as he is on the point of stocking it with furniture, his luck will change. Public taste will shift; his work will no longer be wanted; or perhaps editors who have been buying his material will be replaced by people who have "pets" of their own. The reading public, notoriously fickle, will purchase twenty thousand copies of an author's first book and seven hundred of his second.

Just as the perfume hucksters sell the glamour of Tabu, so the mail-order mesmerizers promote the "glamour" of authorship. Many Americans have been sold the notion that being a successful author is like being a movie star.

The fact is that the majority of writers who earn their living by the pen are not glamorous at all. Nine-tenths of them toil in the outhouses of literature. The pulp magazines overflow with the mass-produced rubbish of writers who began writing for a penny a word in the belief that this was a steppingstone to greater things, and who remained enslaved to the pulps for a lifetime. Indeed, the handful of correspondence-school graduates who succeed in selling their output at all invariably earn their living with the pulps.

These graduates who, at the encouragement of mail-order professors, look forward to enjoying the future as a Hemingway or a Marquand spend their careers turning out pulp adventure stories with locales they never visited, developing characters as true to flesh and blood as matchsticks.

In order to live on the sweatshop fees paid by the pulps, these mechanics have to pound out a million words a year, usually under the stimulus of the bottle, a continual writing jag which saps their creative energy long before its legitimate time. Younger, more energetic writers take their place; they are forced to descend the scale of magazine rates, taking half a cent and even less for a word, until they become animal fodder like horses who have outlived their usefulness.

Occasionally, in an attempt to elude their fate, they take editorial jobs in the only field they know—the pulps. They are virtually chained to a desk, reading an endless procession of manuscripts, as well as editing copy on the drivel already purchased, until they are ready to go berserk or blind. If they aren't thrown out of their jobs by a sudden drop in circulation (the mortality rate in the field is notorious), these editors eventually flee from the sanctum and go back to their writing, preferring to toil at least in a sweatshop of their own creation.

For pulpsters, the ascent to the decently paying slick magazines is nearly unattainable; not one in a hundred become slick writers. But there is one thing in common to professional writing, whether it be of pulp or Nobel Prize quality—the sweat that goes into it.

The correspondence-school soothsayers soft-pedal the agonizing work that is the professional writer's lot. For every ten novices who learn to write competently, only one has the tenacity to stick to the grind. As one veteran author remarked to a literary aspirant, "There's a much tougher trick than getting published—that's *staying* published."

Oscar Wilde, attending a weekend house party, asked his hostess if he might be excused so that he could retire to his writing. He disappeared into his room in the morning and didn't emerge until suppertime. When his hostess asked him what he had accomplished, he replied, "This morning I put a comma in one of my poems; this afternoon I took it out again." William Faulkner once declared that he wrote only when the spirit moved him—and the spirit moved him every day. He meant that a professional writer doesn't wait for inspiration—he *forces* it.

To return to the correspondence schools and the false hopes they engender: It is untrue that they or any other agency can mass-produce writers who will earn big money. However, writing schools, in catering to the greed of the novice by holding out the promise of a fortune to be made, do not, I think, appreciate the fact that the majority of writers who stick to the game despite its frustrations are not lured primarily by money. If a fortune were the lure, they would have quit long ago. There is a much more fundamental attraction. Don Marquis put it graphically. "It isn't the money that makes people write; it is the *hope of publication.* The exhibition of the ego in public places means more to us writers than money. Those lonely, timid, fine souls who write and never show it to any human being at all, show it to God; they are the supreme egotists. They think nobody else would appreciate it."

The urge to be published is a powerful one; and it is endemic in writers regardless of their skill, their reputation, their financial standing. Even old war horses who boast of a dozen published books look forward to their newest appearance in print with the goose pimples of a school girl receiving her first kiss.

Indeed, because big-money authors are so few, they are driven by editors and agents alike to rewrite continually their first successes. Once they succeed with a red-hot formula, they are committed to a life of hasty repeat writing. A telling characteristic of even our greatest novelists—as critics have observed—is that their characters "are profoundly conceived and hastily set down." Modern American literature would lose very little if its most successful novelists were known only by their first books. The number who have matured beyond these is in my opinion negligible.

This lashing of the writer to the wheel of big business is not an exclusive phenomenon of the twentieth century. Dickens was compelled, during lean years, to write advertising copy for an insurance company; Lafcadio Hearn prepared publicity for cotton-growers in the 1880's; Sherwood Anderson wrote food ads.

The struggle between the two selves of an author—his fanciful ego and the practical self fashioned by the economic demands of living—has nowhere been better described than by James M. Barrie, the playwright. With his Scottish sense of humor, Barrie made the artist out to be the black sheep. "McConnachie . . . is the name I give to the unruly half of myself. . . . We are complement and supplement. I am the half that is dour and practical and canny; he is the fanciful half; my desire is to be the family solicitor, standing firm on my hearth-rug among the hard realities of the office furniture, while he prefers to fly around on one wing. I should not mind him doing that, but he drags me with him! . . . He has clung to me, less from mischief than for companionship. I half like him and his penny whistle. With all his faults he is as Scotch as peat."

Just as the writer is beset by conflict, so the society that molded him is hard-pressed by its contradictory aspects. There is, on the one hand, the dog-eat-dog struggle we carry on in the market place, and, on the other hand, the concern we express for the Russians, the Chinese and the Chaco Indians who do not enjoy the blessings of our American democracy. We pay lip service to the holiness of American motherhood, and spend vast sums of money for plays, books and magazines saturated with polite pornography. Indeed, *Life,* our leading picture magazine, continually revels in sex served up as sociological inquiry.

This sanctimoniousness reminds me of a letter a reader sent to Sherwood Anderson, one of our literary pioneers in sex. "I adore your story, 'I'm a Fool,' " she wrote. "But I detest your novel, 'Many Marriages.' How could you ever have written such a filthy book? You must have a rotten mind. I admire you tremendously. Please send me an autographed photo and your signature." Yes, many Americans, though they have thrown off their belief in God, still believe passionately in the devil.

The American writer, whether wet-nursed in a correspondence school or feeling his oats as a published author, is hard-pressed by modern society to be pretentious instead of sincere, to be elaborately outré instead of the normal man he is. Once he achieves publication, he counts his blessings in literary cocktail parties sometimes more than in laudatory reviews. Indeed, the cocktail party was established specifically to cater to his vanity (and to the egos of the snobs who itch to shake hands with him). It is really something to observe the homage paid a behemoth with rumpled hair and tremendous hands, who looks like a butcher but is the author of the latest sociological novel.

Most publishers are irritated at having to tolerate this flimflammery, but since it comes under the heading of keeping an author happy, they go through with it. I once cornered at one of these parties a publishing executive who explained to me, "I go to them because they come at the right time of the day. At this hour I would ordinarily be signing my mail; and if I am out of my office, I am absolved of all responsibility for what goes on in the organization."

The urge to be published and to enjoy the adulation that goes with it is the lodestone that produces manuscripts: but tragically few receive the accolade. Few authors can live by their writing alone, and the writing of books, because the average financial returns are so small, has become a prestige-builder when it is not simply an avocation. Yet even writers who live by the pen alone sometimes come to the subsidy publisher.

Life in the co-operative publishing business is real, and

God knows it is earnest, and as a poet of slightly less stature than Longfellow, one George M. Cohan, remarked, it is also "a very funny proposition after all." After twenty years of it I can still laugh and cry, and that's something nowadays to brag about.

CHAPTER XIII

How to Lose a Million Dollars

The people you meet and the friendships you make are the richest rewards of publishing. If I didn't have the Authors' League to keep me in line, I know I still would follow the code I drew up when I began. This is not the *non sequitur* it may seem. The Authors' League is the lion of literature; once a publisher is downed by these doughty lads there's nothing left but the last rites, and these won't save him from eternal damnation. But one day I risked this because I wanted to add one special book to my 1955 list, even though the list had already been set at 233 by tight production schedules.

President of the league, at this moment, is the famous Rex Stout, creator of Nero and Archie. This had special significance that morning (I remember that one of the hurricanes was blowing) after I had waited in my office for a lady who had given me a rendezvous at 9 A.M. As a bachelor publisher I have learned that these early-morning appointments are rarely kept, especially by younger authors. I had never met this lady, but she had had, on the telephone, a young and pleasant voice; I was agreeably surprised when she arrived, on the dot, and proved to be the spriest grandmother this side of Hollywood.

She had a book on mulch gardening that needed only a title to be popular. I suggested *How to Have a Green Thumb Without an Aching Back,* and she said that would do fine. We agreed on terms, and it was then that Ruth Stout told me that her brother is Rex Stout, a man with the passionate belief that any money passing between author and publisher should go from right to left. *This* money was going the wrong way.

I was scared. Every publisher the manuscript had been submitted to turned it down on grounds that it wouldn't sell. Supposing they were right? Supposing my organization failed to sell a book written by the sister of the authors' watchdog? The hurricane that howled outside did not compare with the turmoil going on inside me.

I picked up the manuscript and looked through it again. I knew very little about gardening, but it was apparent to me that Miss Stout knew a great deal and, what was more important, had the knack of being able to impart her knowledge to others in an entertaining way. And I looked at the dust clouds billowing outside the window and thought of the thousands of devotees in their precious few yards of soil to whom the appearance of the first lettuce or the triumphant flowering of a zinnia was poetry come to life.

I thought of these things and I turned to Miss Stout and I was Lindbergh taking off for Paris. "Okay," I said, "let's go."

Nero Wolfe never made a suspect sweat half as much as I was sweating then, though of course I don't suppose Miss Stout suspected a thing. Come to think of it, though, she did have a twinkle in her eye. Maybe she had heard her brother on the subject of paying for publication. . . .

At this writing her book is selling well, magazines have reprinted sections, reviews are very good, Miss Stout has difficulty replying to her enthusiastic mail, and only the manufacturers of synthetic fertilizers are sour. Mulch, mulch, mulch, the boys (and girls) are mulching, and I doubt if Mr. Stout will send Archie here.

The best safeguard for the publisher of a book of apparently limited appeal is to issue a small first edition. For example, Simon and Schuster's first printing of Will Durant's *Story of Philosophy* (perhaps because it was subsidized by the author) was 1,500 copies, though it became one of the big nonfiction sellers of this century. Dutton ordered a first printing of only 500 copies of *The Story of San Michele;* before the year was out it had passed fifty editions. Dale Carnegie's *How to Win Friends and Influence People* was issued in a first edition of only 3,000 copies by S. and S.

The adaptation of this and other special publishing techniques have in recent years made subsidy publishing successful for the first time in actually *publishing* books—a term which must include distribution and sales as well as book production. Nevertheless, I have been criticized, even lambasted, by interested parties for accepting money to issue books—at the same time that they were competing among themselves to snare subsidies on certain titles.

Subsidy publishers have been criticized adversely on the theory that no subsidized book is legitimate except when the book is issued by a trade publisher. Shortly after I first organized Exposition Press, the New York *Daily Mirror* claimed that the business was simply a scheme for separating poets from their money, at the same time neglecting to mention that for the fee the poet was rendered a service: for only three dollars he and his verse were published and he received a copy of the anthology. However, the article had no ill effect that I could see. Not a single poet who had paid me requested a refund. On the other hand, I received letters from three people who wished to have their verse published. One of them wrote, "I saw your advertisement [*sic!*] in the *Daily Mirror* and I am sending you two of my poems. If you will publish at least one of them, you can rest assured that I will buy a copy of your book."

In publishing the useful book with a limited audience, I

sometimes have been approached with curious propositions. After I sent the author a contract quoting the publication price for a manuscript on buttonhook collecting, she hinted that I should be happy to publish the book for a song, if I could find it in my heart to charge her anything at all, because the manuscript was of transcendent importance. Was I aware that there were only six buttonhook collectors in the entire world, and that she was giving me first chance at a definite work on the subject? Though I am sympathetic to small audiences, there is a limit to my bias. It occurred to me that an audience of six readers was slicing it rather thin, and I suggested that the lady would be better off mailing her typewritten manuscript for each to read in turn.

We have specialized in reaching limited reading audiences; as indicated, trade publishers have been forced into a similar situation for many titles, not by choice but by necessity. Not only is the reading public a small one at best, but it is estimated that only 40 per cent of these readers purchase the books they read; 60 per cent borrow them.

About sixty million Americans live beyond the reach of bookstores. In Nevada, the sixth largest state, there are only two. The Middle West is shockingly undeveloped as a retail market, compared with the east and west coasts. Surveys indicate that the book-club market, far from supplementing the bookstore clientele, is largely an urbanized one, having relatively little effect on the rural population. Incidentally, the membership of book clubs has been falling steadily since the end of World War II. The chief reason people give for canceling their subscription is that they got fed up with the restricted diet handed them. The editors of the Book-of-the-Month Club as individuals have listed their own choice of books, which did not coincide with the selections they made mutually for the club.

One factor which every author insists limits the audience for his books is the publishers' halfhearted advertising policies. Indeed, the failure of publishers to advertise energetically is the author's number-one gripe. I have been bewildered to hear a number of publishers who presumably are in dead earnest about increasing their reading public declare that advertising is virtually useless in selling books; that when they run ads it is chiefly to impress the authors and booksellers.

There may be many reasons why book ads don't sell books. And granted a book has a wide sales potential, the typical book ad may still not pull. I feel that with most ads this is so because (*a*) typographically they are not attractive, (*b*) they don't tell you what the book is about and (*c*) they do not educate the public to want to buy books. Lucky Strikes, for example, have fought, to quote another, to start selling from the cradle. The publishers must find a way to make books as appealing as dolls and toys to children. Book reading should become a lifetime habit. I'd also like to point out that although writers like Mickey Spillane and Joshua Liebman with his *Peace of Mind* rake up hundreds of thousands, if not millions, of people who had not bought a book before, the general public, no matter what their reading level, can be interested in certain types of books, if they are brought to their attention. Certainly they cannot be reached by placing ads in the book sections of newspapers and periodicals which are, of course, ignored in favor of the drama, TV or sports sections.

I must agree with Cheney in his economic survey of the industry that "if ads are run chiefly to impress the author and bookseller, then all advertising should be stopped at once and the money should be distributed among authors and booksellers."

I would say of my experience that it depends upon the book itself as to how much advertising should be done. The only advertising that counts, and the ultimate purpose back of all other advertising, is the word-of-mouth kind. If you open a restaurant and advertise it widely you will get customers—once. You will not get them in again for any money unless you give them food and cooking they like.

It is so with a book. Badly written books, or books of limited appeal, need not and in fact should not be advertised in national media. You might persuade someone to part with three dollars, but if he throws the book away in disgust you have made an enemy for the author and for yourself.

For books which have wide reading appeal or high literary value a reasonable amount of advertising in the book sections of the larger newspapers and in some of the better trade magazines may pay because these advertisements are read by booksellers and the section of the public that is book-minded.

It is an indisputable fact that book publishers do not advertise in the most expensive advertising media, such as the *Saturday Evening Post, Collier's* or *Life* magazine. Of course, the question poses itself whether or not these ads fail to pay because there is no market or because the merchandising is not of top-notch caliber. I am of the opinion that the merchandising technique of the publishing field is very poor, and I base this on what I would presume to call logic. Almost every large corporation has at one time or another been cited by the Better Business Bureau and the Federal Trade Commission for writing copy that was "too hot." These eminently respectable firms evidently go all out in trying to sell a product. At times their selling enthusiasm appears to go out of bounds and they have to be pulled into line again. Publishers have rarely been called to task for writing copy which was conceivably too enthusiastic. It is regrettable that the only time a publisher gets into trouble with the Federal Trade Commission or the postal authorities is because he inadvertently, or perhaps deliberately, allows the proverbial fig leaf to slip out of position.

But there are many forms of advertising which are more effective. Some mass-produced books of a specialized nature have been sold at bargain rates over the radio, but no novel ever has been sold in this way. Window displays are extremely effective but have a limited and localized appeal. Outdoor advertising (i.e., posters and billboards) would cost disproportionately to its value. However, cards in trains and buses can sell books, because the traveler is in a receptive mood for reading. Bookstores on the big liners have always done well.

Regional books should be announced in the most effective media of the region, and specialized books, such as Miss Stout's useful book on mulch gardening, should be promoted in suburban areas and large cities and will do better there than in the country, where farmers think they know all the tricks.

The best advertising is word-of-mouth. It has made all the best-sellers. And the second best is free publicity, the notice a worth-while book will receive in newspapers and magazines if it is properly called to the attention of reviewers and other feature writers. Next to production itself, my publicity department is the biggest single item in the budget for each book.

Publishers place over 60 per cent of their ads in the New York *Times* and the New York *Herald Tribune*. New York represents 40 per cent of the national retail book market. Granting the fact that these newspapers have a circulation beyond the Hudson, the disproportionate amount of advertising concentrated in a single city and in a single medium is, to me, unhealthy.

It is a carry-over in this country from England, where three great newspapers, the *Times,* the *Sunday-Times* and the *Ob-*

server, are read by a vast literary-minded public. But these newspapers are read throughout the British Isles; their appeal is to 60,000,000 potential buyers, not 10,000,000. There are no national newspapers in this country in any way comparable with the great English ones. Only one American newspaper circulates throughout the United States, the *Christian Science Monitor* of Boston. *Monitor* reviews are excellent—for certain books.

I have said before and I repeat, there is a tremendous undeveloped market for books in the United States. But to reach it publishers must carry their message to the hinterland.

Concentration of the industrial publishing plant here has resulted in the centralization of credit in New York banks. This has caused a top-heavy credit structure; firms are placed in needless competition with each other. And, sadly enough, publishers have very low credit standings. An inventory of stock in most other businesses has banks competing to make loans because the collateral is fixed in value. But a publisher's collateral is books, and the whim of the public can reduce a five-dollar best-seller to a nickel remainder.

I know of a publisher whose records showed that he sold a quarter of a million dollars' worth of books annually over a ten-year period, but his bank, when he approached them, would offer only $5,000 and that only if he pledged all his stock as security. To the banking barons books are packaged dreams that have no value on the auction block. They will lend $100,000 to finance the production of a new hair-curler or can-opener but will not risk a dollar on a promising book list.

The public can be reached and can be sold. More than ten million copies of the Bible were sold by a five-and-ten store chain. And who goes to the five-and-ten for divine guidance? They were, I believe, produced for five cents a copy and sold for fifteen cents, but that was a quarter of a century ago when all publishing costs were about a fifth of their present figure.

When a writer comes to me with a book that has a small audience potential, he is under no illusion that he will become rich on royalties—or if he has such illusions it is my job to dispel them. But trade books, since they are published for profit, start on a different basis; many an author, hearing of the opulence of a few lucky writers and observing the widespread distribution of their books, luxuriates in rosy dreams about his own prospects. He could have saved himself heartaches had he had a prior talk with a bookseller.

The bookseller would, or could, tell him what a shockingly large number of titles sell practically nothing beyond their advance sale and how publishers, once they have dumped an edition on the retailer's counter, wash their hands of the matter. And he will tell him how little he as a bookseller can do for most books unless the publisher gets behind it with an aggressive merchandising campaign.

Year after year publishers go through the same elaborate tactics of high-pressuring the bookseller. They send bright young salesmen with lavishly illustrated catalogues and colorful jackets to try to overload the outlets with as large an advance sale as possible, knowing that in many cases this will delude the bookdealers into representing it as a best-seller.

The hocus-pocus with which publishers conjure up books but fail miserably to make them disappear brings to mind a story about a circus barker who met a woman who owned a lunchroom that was a business flop. She couldn't get customers into her place. The barker placed a large bowl of water in the window. Beside it he put up a cardboard sign reading, "Here is the only living Tasmanian fish in captivity." In a corner, out of sight, he placed an electric fan that blew ripples on the water. In no time at all, a crowd gathered at the window. "See the fish? There it goes," boomed the barker, and the people craned their necks, ohing and ahing at the movements of the invisible fish.

However, unlike the uninformed public, many booksellers have developed sharp eyes and an excellent smell for fish stories. Even the incomparable Knopf lamented that he wouldn't get the next book of Nicholas Monsarrat (author of a previous best-seller), because the bookstores had returned for credit half the books sold in advance of publication. And, *gentle* man that he is, remarked, "And it is the rare author who does not blame his publisher when the fate of his book is not a happy one."

Nevertheless, despite the bluff and confusion on Parnassus, despite faulty advertising, the bottleneck of distribution, the locust swarm of "ten-percenters" who fasten on the established writer's pocketbook and the sharks who trim him when he first starts out, authors will continue to write. They will go on writing because they cannot help themselves. The teacher, the librarian, the bank teller, the sea captain and the cowboy will continue to set down on paper ideas they believe are peculiar to themselves. The writer who has already published and gone broke on his book will sweat over a new tome, hoping that this one will be the lucky strike. The select few who have reached the top will continue to grind out their pemmican.

And this is as it should be. Writing a book is a harmless indoor sport, and even paying for its publication costs a lot less than a great many other indulgences that lack half the satisfaction and pride that a book can give. Looked at in one light, the writing of books can be a great national virtue. When a man is writing a book he may be hard to talk to while he's working, but at least his wife knows where he is at night.

CHAPTER XIV

Hollywood B.O.

As with most publishers, my life has had its share of disappointments and anticlimaxes. I have had my visions and ideals. But this is the age of the Philistine, when the artistic, the bold, the unpredictable, must end with a moral. Only we spell "moral" a little differently: we spell it "box office."

I grew to manhood in a New York that rapidly was losing its horse-drawn culture. Its literary purlieus were no longer centered about the Athenian art for art's sake. The change was nowhere more noticeable, of course, than in Greenwich Village, where in my salad days I coffeed with Clement Wood, Henry Harrison and other bohemians. The intellectual barricades were falling; conversation was a lost art; the huddle in the corner was not an argument for and against Dada but a short-haired girl telling a dirty story. By the time I made my pilgrimage to the Village bistros the squeamish and the fastidious had long abandoned the fort and the young Davids had surrendered to Goliath and were nursing paunches in advertising or motion-picture studios. Vice in the Village was no longer gilded with talent and its homosexuality was unmitigated by wit.

With the Village reduced to the status of a backyard of Bellevue, the genuine writers and artists kept to themselves or moved out to Greenwich, Connecticut, to write slick nothings that helped fill their swimming pools. New York culture lost its iconoclasm. The intelligentsia not only had taken to wearing ties but were going to Charvet for them, and they got their hair cut once a fortnight.

The day was gone when literary fashion could be set by Heywood Broun roaming through the Algonquin with a hole in his pants. The unruly years were over. Harold Ross's shoe-brush hair began to lie down flat. And even if George S. Kaufman's thatch remained wild, he at least could boast a solid-gold Cadillac.

When I entered publishing, I was susceptible enough to be impressed by the new Brooks Brothers highbrows, who talked endlessly about their psychoanalysis and the natural history of their glands. I found that the wealthier they were the more furiously they espoused radical causes, as if to relieve their guilt for succumbing to the box office. But whatever their qualms, they wisecracked and tom-catted their way through boredom, changing sexual partners more frequently than they once had changed their underwear.

But if the flag of the New York intelligentsia had been flying at half mast since the frolics of the Algonquin Round Table, the standards of Hollywood have remained the same since the birth of the nickelodeon. As my publishing interests grew and I required a Hollywood office, I found refugees from Greenwich, Connecticut, days lounging beside even larger swimming pools. While the easy money they had received for being slick back East had driven them to champion socialism, the greater sums they now netted for doing even less had turned them toward explorations of the subconscious. To assuage their sense of guilt, they drank more between meals, played poker for higher stakes, lived on benzedrine and drove their over-worked glands to further records of endurance.

I watched Hollywood develop through the antics of these *émigrés.* As the movies grew from peanuts to pearls, Hollywood signified a new way of life as lavish as that enjoyed by Romans during a similarly decadent era. Bathrooms changed from "cans" to *salons d'art,* one lady having a room for her ablutions walled, ceilinged and floored by mirrors. As the movies progressed from smell to sound, writers who could really write on paper as well as their cuffs were imported at a cheering rate. In 1930 anyone who had ever published a book could get a job, and a piano salesman sold a thousand pianos to a single studio; they called it the Gold Rush.

During a party I attended at which producers, stars and writers were bowing before an altar crowded with cocktails and canapés I overheard one director speak very animatedly to a producer. The producer shook his head.

"The story's no good. No drama in it."

"What do you mean—no drama?" yelled the director, outraged.

"Nobody is enough of a bastard to get killed."

Along with the great new sound stages, scores of beaverboard cages were built for the writers. One studio alone hired two hundred new writers in a six-month period. A producer in this studio read a book by an English writer and went to London to seek the genius out in person. He couldn't find him. He never did find him. The British scholar had been sitting out a contract in the producer's own Culver City studio; when his option came up and nobody had given him an assignment he went back to England.

Pelham G. Wodehouse, "Plum" to his friends, went to Paramount on a short-term contract and wrote an entire script the first weekend he was there. The boys at the Writers' Club on Sunset Boulevard were horrified. Their habit when getting an assignment was to go to Mexico duck-hunting for the first two months, and never, never show up with a finished script until the last day of the contract. The Englishman hadn't played cricket. When he was proposed for membership there were a dozen blackballs.

Another writer told members of the same club at an open meeting that he was completely sold on a movie career. "I've had fifty-two weeks at Metro so far," he said, "and only written ten pages—a letter home." The boys were again scandalized. These were things you didn't *say*. "If this keeps up," said Rupert Hughes, president of the club, "they'll have us all *working*."

Writers never had it so good. Expatriates from Greenwich, Connecticut, and Macdougal Alley were collectively nostalgic about their attic days in Montparnasse but had no objection to living almost as well as the illiterates who owned the studios. And the more swimming pools they built, the bitterer became their resentment; and a few now knew that although you can't eat integrity it is possible to die for its loss.

It was always with a sense of relief that I returned to New York after these Hollywood visits. The neon lights of Broadway are comforting after the klieg lights of California. New York is still a community of individuals. We still have our *boulevardiers,* though shorn of spats and cane, and one may be unconventional here without becoming a beachcomber.

I felt my way through and around the world of professional writing, more and more disconcerted at the lack of sincerity everywhere. There is a real story in every life if it could be told; what we have been getting are repeats of previous successes. There may be only seven plots. I don't know. It would seem to me that an age that can invent an atom bomb ought to be able to invent one new plot.

But it is a fact that a story depends on its sincerity more than on its actual writing. I was acquainted with a wealthy paralytic who was confined to a wheel chair and the attentions of the beautiful brunette he had married. He became a successful novelist; and his wife not only lived up to her loyalties; she was his business agent as well. She fed the invalid kindness and morphine and sat hour after hour by his bedside when he was not obliged to play his role of stimulating host, which he loved.

I happened to know this woman's story. She had been on the streets when my friend met and married her, boosting her into society and buying her a crested mink. She nursed him eight years and in his last hour the paralytic kissed her and cried exultantly, "At last I'm going to be well!"

Three weeks after the burial of her husband the devoted widow was arrested on suspicion of having hastened his end by administering an overdose of sleeping pills. There was a division of opinion as to whether she had killed him to hasten his release or the collection of her inheritance.

I took her side. The predicament this woman was in appealed to my sentimentality. I persuaded her to write her own story, believing that it would be a valuable document for psychologists and the lay reader alike. She accepted my suggestion and wrote her book, in which she defended herself with ability but a complete lack of sincerity.

It was only when I read her manuscript that I changed my opinion about her motives. I knew now why my friend had died.

The art of autobiography is a rare gift. It is nearly impossible to write the truth about oneself—the whole truth, without embroidery. Try it and see. If you are honest you will find you have created a fictional character called "I."

If it is hard for a man to write the truth about himself it is doubly difficult for a woman, because a woman lives in a much more artificial world with personal vanity playing a much bigger part than it does with a man. Even Ilka Chase hasn't equaled in frankness—or anywhere near it—the confessions of Frank Harris or Rousseau. It is only when a woman writes about another woman that she can be cruel.

From my office I have had a view of the shifting scene of characters spinning around the merry-go-round, be they beautiful wives who have given their husbands an overdose of sleeping pills, alcoholic portrait painters commuting between Bellevue and Mexico City, or successful businessmen turned autobiographers who write nostalgically of how they made their millions on a shoestring. I have had dealings with authors who kept furiously trying to milk the teat of a muse that had grown so dry it had long since forgotten the memory of motherhood. I have met, on the other hand, skillful ladies whose writings were often better, sometimes worse, but never quite so old as they were.

One of my authors was a grade B movie star by vocation. I used to discuss her manuscripts with her in a West Side bistro against the background of melodies from a gypsy orchestra. She loved to startle her visitors by receiving them while soaping herself in her bathtub; smoked Corona cigars; once to shock a group of newly made acquaintances, she handed a twenty-dollar bill to a drunken panhandler who, she insisted, was her first lover. She insisted on introducing her young escorts as her illegitimate sons at parties and having herself introduced as "Miss —— and her child." This queen wrote and sold fiction to religious and family magazines, which epitomized all the virtues she scorned.

But even virtue has a naïveté that is often misunderstood, as was the roommate of a model I knew. The model supplemented her meager income by posing as co-respondent for a "specialist" who manufactured photographic evidence for quick divorces. One evening when she was busy on another job, she talked her roommate into taking her place. "After all," she argued, "all you have to do is pose in your slip with a man in shirtsleeves." But the clincher was the $25 fee, which in those depression days was a handsome contribution to the roommate's dowry.

As the scene was later being enacted before a photographer at the other end of the room, in walked the roommate's fiance, who stopped short, turned white and beat a wordless, furious retreat. The frightened roommate clattered down the stairs from the fourth-floor walkup screaming, "Honey, honey, you don't understand—I'm only doing it for the money!"

My life has been a continual struggle of adjustment. As a child I had to adjust to a physical handicap, to poverty and to living in a neighborhood seething with racial hatred. As I reached adolescence I had to adjust to the additional humiliations brought on by the depression.

Lacking a formal education, I entered publishing as an outsider and every step forward was a struggle to gain recognition. My parents had a strong instinct for moral living, and the ethics they taught me I have found since to be the permanent values. Dignity is a precious thing, and a bad conscience is a sure breeder of ulcers. What is also important is that ethics and a full belly can live together.

CHAPTER XV

Faith, Fate and Foibles

Some curbstone philosopher has remarked that only a nickel's worth of iodine in the thyroid gland prevents a man from turning into a gibbering idiot. And no men better illustrate the narrow dividing line between pomposity and cretinism than some of the pedagogic Pecksniffians of the publishing business. You sound mad, Mr. Uhlan. Well, I am mad.

You see, I regard the business I am in as in the nature of a public service. The attitude of the trade, of *Publishers' Weekly* and of newspapers toward all subsidy publishing was justified at one time. It is outdated now. The hard fact that the trade publishers cannot publish one-tenth of the books that deserve and ought to be published makes my business a necessity. The function of the publisher is to add to the world's entertainment and learning by publishing books. There is an obligation on the industry to publish *all* worth-while books. Trade publishers cannot in these days fulfill that obligation because if they did they'd all go broke.

That's where subsidy publishers come in, and I have the conviction that we are as necessary to the publishing business itself as we are to the authors who otherwise would not see their books in print.

In the course of this book I have freely admitted the faults of the subsidy-publishing houses, and I have been frank about my own methods of correcting them. A chief complaint used to concern the fact that subsidy houses turned out technically sloppy books, badly bound and printed and teeming with misprints.* As a matter of fact, mistakes in first editions are so common that the rare-book business is largely built on them. The author who comes upon a typographical error in his first book can take comfort from the fact that if it ever becomes successful a small error may enhance its value.

The very fact that this complaint against subsidy publishers was justified makes me go to extraordinary pains to see that the quality of workmanship in Exposition books is of a consistently high level. The more books we can sell, the more money we, as well as our authors, will make, and I know that shoddy-looking books don't sell.

If the necessity for subsidy publishing is patent now, there always was a case to be made out for it. The Tarzan stories, to take one instance, would never have delighted the millions they have if publication had been dependent on the trade. Edgar Rice Burroughs organized his own publishing firm, sold 20,000,000 copies and built a California town from the profits. To my knowledge, Tarzana is the only town ever named after a character in fiction.

In 1906, Upton Sinclair wrote his first notable novel, *The Jungle,* a shocking exposé of the American Beef Trust. When President Theodore Roosevelt read Sinclair's description of how millions of pounds of tubercular and gangrenous meat were being sold annually to the American people, he launched an investigation of the Chicago stockyards. Within six months after the publication of *The Jungle,* Congress passed laws revamping the meat industry, and one of the most notable victories ever achieved by the pen was recorded.

---

* There were 150 errors in spelling in the first edition of F. Scott Fitzgerald's *This Side of Paradise,* published not by a subsidy house but by the venerable house of Scribner.

However, the Beef Trust, Wall Street and other pillars of monopoly capital were infuriated. Even while Sinclair was writing his novel, he was a marked man. The meat packers tried to bribe him to quit. Failing in this, they tried to persuade his publishers not to bring the book out. They filled the press with lies about Sinclair and threatened newspapers with reprisals if his novel was reviewed.

A few more thrusts at business in his novels, and Sinclair was tossed to the lions by the publishing industry. His obvious commercial value was outweighed in the fine scales of publishing psychology by his "dangerous radicalism." Sinclair had to underwrite his own books for the next twenty-five years. Only recently was he taken under the wing of Viking, after he had faded into respectability with the passing of time.

Incidentally, for any reader who may have the urge to follow Sinclair's profession of martyrdom, a self-appraisal of what it cost the writer to accumulate his equipment may be illuminating. "I have been fifteen years in getting the education to write *The Jungle,*" he declared shortly after its publication. "During twelve of these years I have actually been practicing at writing, and during that time I have written not less than five million words. During the same time I have read certainly four or five thousand books, including all the worthwhile novels in the five languages which I succeeded in acquiring. . . . To enable me to write the first chapter [a musical scene] I had to spend nearly three years studying the violin and to attend many hundreds of concerts. To enable me to write other portions of the book, I had to get married and become a father. The cost of the whole equipment would certainly not have been less than $20,000."

When the protectors of the public morals on Mount Parnassus have breathed dragon flames at me and my subsidy colleagues, when the *Literary Market Place,* blue book of the industry, declined to list me as one of its own and I was refused advertising in *Publishers' Weekly,* I couldn't help recalling that the classic instance of business chicanery was achieved not by the subsidy publishers but among the high and the mighty. I refer to the historic case of Charles Sheldon.

Sheldon was a Protestant minister who, discouraged by poor attendance in his church, hit upon the plan of delivering his sermons in the form of serial fiction whose characters and plots would illustrate his moral lessons. Each Sunday he broke off a chapter at the most exciting point, and he packed the pews. One such successful serial, *In His Steps,* dealt with the efforts of an American community to put the principles of Jesus into its day-by-day living. This serial engendered so much enthusiasm in his congregation that Sheldon persuaded a trade publisher to issue it as a book. The publisher made a blunder in arranging for the copyright; instead of depositing two copies with the copyright department in Washington, as the law required, he filed only a single copy. As a result the book was thrown into the public domain.

In His Steps sold like wildfire. In less than a year sixteen different American publishers pounced upon it because of its defective copyright, and issued pirated editions. The original publisher, in the meantime, got into financial difficulties and was forced into bankruptcy, selling the plates to a competitor.

One would think that the other publishers would have been actuated by a sense of decency, even if under no legal compulsion, to send Sheldon royalties. But most did nothing of the sort. The author, who was badly in need of funds, was later contacted by a movie company who wanted to make the book into a film, but the receivers of the bankrupt publisher, getting wind of the offer, threatened to sue Sheldon, claiming the movie rights to the book had passed into their hands with the receivership. They had no legal case whatsoever, but the incredibly naïve author borrowed five hundred dollars and paid them to drop their suit. Almost immediately, the film company folded and the negotiations fell through.

To date, Sheldon's *In His Steps* has sold close to thirty million copies. Next to the Bible and Shakespeare, it is believed to be the top-selling book of all time. It has been translated into dozens of languages and hawked all over the world. Once when Sheldon traveled to Haifa, Palestine, a missionary came up to him with a copy of the book in Arabic which he declared was being read in every Mohammedan country. On another occasion Sheldon stopped at an inn in New Zealand, where a barmaid pointed to his book between bottles of whisky and gin, announcing that she was reading it "between drinks." In Australia, a bookstore clerk told Sheldon, "We have sold a hundred and fifty thousand copies of your book; we cannot get additional copies fast enough." This was the first indication Sheldon received that the book had been published in Australia. The Melbourne publisher had simply pirated a London publisher's edition and had put his own copyright on it.

A tradesman in Glasgow put out an edition, printing the name of his store on every page, and it turned out to be one of the most profitable ads ever issued. A British publisher put out a low-priced edition and sold two million copies. His conscience bothered him to the extent that he sent Sheldon a hundred dollars. The book was published in Soviet Russia, but the translator, afraid to disclose his name in connection with a religious project, wrote on the title-page, "Translated by nobody." An Armenian translation had to wait several years for the censor's approval because certain passages offended his government.

When an edition was planned for Argentina, the translator wrote Sheldon that he was going to change the names of the characters, since they were hard for Spanish people to pronounce. When Sheldon received a copy he was amazed to find that the name of his hero, Henry Maxwell, the minister, had been changed to Henry Ford. When he wrote a letter of complaint, the translator retorted, "I am very sorry, Mr. Sheldon, but the truth is that Henry FORD is better known down here than Henry MAXWELL."

Not only did Sheldon receive no royalties, but he went through a great deal of difficulty to secure copies of most of the foreign translations; the publishers didn't even have the decency to provide him with copies. There was, however, one exception to this general rule of chicanery. One publisher out of the forty who reaped the profits of Sheldon's book voluntarily sent him royalties on two editions. This was Grosset & Dunlap. The others took the unbusinesslike minister for one of the most spectacular sleigh rides in publishing history, exploiting a book that, ironically, preached the application of Christ's teachings in the modern business world!

Admittedly, this is an extreme case of publishing malfeasance. The ethics of the trade publisher are on the whole high for the age we live in. Nevertheless—and this is illuminating—orthodox publishers are plagued by even stronger guilt feelings in the carrying on of their trade than they attribute to the unregenerate subsidy houses. There are dilettante publishers who picture themselves as aristocrats who have been forced by the facts of life into sullying their hands in the dishwater of commerce. They are revolted at the idea of being identified with the American business community.

Curiously enough, the American intelligentsia—our writers, historians, social essayists—have traditionally pictured the businessman as the villain in our society. In the early part of the century, Ida M. Tarbell, Frank Norris and Lincoln Steffens lambasted the American capitalist, and there has been little disposition to let up on him today. Frederick Wakeman's *The Hucksters,* and even J. P. Marquand's sly lampoons, follow the tradition.

The irony is that big business has undergone a drastic change in function since the days of the robber barons. With the dispersal of corporate ownership into the hands of numerous stockholders and the passing of administrative control from the founder-owners into the keeping of a professional managerial class whose motives are much more enlightened than those of the classic economic man, business has developed a sense of responsibility to society that is a far cry from the days of untamed rugged individualism. Public-opinion polls reveal that the business executive today is frequently more internationally minded than his workers. He has been a more enthusiastic supporter of the Marshall Plan and Point Four aid to undeveloped peoples than many of the union members in his plant.

The fact is that while the finicky lords of publishing hesitate to "lower" themselves into the category of businessmen, today's business leaders have assumed virtually all the markings of professional men. It is no longer a question of whether big business is socially acceptable to Mount Parnassus, but whether publishers possess enough acumen to be welcomed into the aristocracy of big business. The paradox of the American Babbitt's gaining in stature while the Thinker has been losing his is an epic switch on the theme of Anatole France's *Thaïs,* wherein a holy monk who is sent to save the soul of a prostitute succumbs to the fleshpots and turns into a panderer while the whore becomes a saint.

Actually there is no reason today for the intelligentsia to keep up the pretense of exclusive status. A missionary nun wouldn't remain a virgin for long if she had to take up quarters in a Chinese house of joy. What has happened to the American intellectual over the past fifty years is exactly what happens to the white man who lives among bushmen. He gradually goes native under the influence of the environment. Somerset Maugham has vividly described how Englishmen who are sent to South Sea outposts as engineers or plantation supervisors guard against deterioration, at first, by shaving meticulously for dinner each evening and dressing in ceremonial whites. But as time goes on, the jungle gets them; they take a native woman to bed, father black children, eventually go around unshaven in a sweaty open shirt and shorts. Unless they are recalled to England before it is too late, the environment completely wins out over them.

And so, today's intellectual, who once may have sat at the feet of William James and regarded learning with reverence, pops up as a quiz panelist, outmugging Groucho Marx for the makers of cheeses and salad dressings or scribbling an *Outline of Knowledge* for bootblacks.

One indication of the decline of American culture has been marked by the emergence of Dale Carnegie, who has fertilized the American prairies with educational bandysham. Carnegie's attitude toward life is eloquent: whenever in doubt, pull a dollar bill out of your pocket, look at George Washington and ask him how *he* would have handled your problem. Carnegie's *How to Win Friends and Influence People* is a distillation of the philosophy of Plato, Benjamin Franklin, Frank Woolworth, Mary Pickford and Bernard Baruch's maid. It is small wonder, with the lucrative premiums that have been placed upon the miscegenation of knowledge, that other writers have followed Carnegie's example, plowing through culture like studding bulls.

Yet, despite the fact that the intelligentsia has yielded to the *Jacquerie,* a number of individuals have done so with extreme reluctance, clinging stubbornly—in private—to the shreds of illusion. Will Durant, who made more money performing as an educator for the masses than most other writers of his time, has expressed his intellectual preference for a monarchy. "In a monarchy," he declared, "you have only to educate one man, the king, to get superior government; in a democracy you have got to educate the masses—an impossible task."

Hendrik Willem Van Loon, Durant's twin who ruled the firmament of mass education, also had a pretty low opinion of the millions who fed him. Van Loon was an inveterate snob who fancied himself to be a reincarnation of Erasmus, the sixteenth-century Dutch scholar. For fifteen years Van Loon had a hard time making a living, until he suddenly stumbled upon a vein he was thoroughly equipped to exploit—the insatiable hunger of Americans for fiction cooked up as fact, for knowledge stewed in the juices of confessionals.

This intellectual, billed by his publisher as the dean of cultural democrats, boasted constantly of his friendship with Queen Wilhelmina and other bluebloods, and took the entire world for his province, writing of history as though it were his intimate diary. He compressed the happenings of centuries into a folksy paragraph, and aeons into a lilting page. Whether he wrote about the times of Socrates, the hanging gardens of Nebuchadnezzar, the Crusades, or the Industrial Revolution, Van Loon was the leading protagonist of his re-creation.

He wrote a story of Rembrandt which was the autobiography of Hendrik Willem Van Loon, with a few facts about the painter casually thrown in. Upon beginning a book on Beethoven, he wrote his publisher, "There won't be much about Beethoven in it. He's not very interesting. I think I'll make it my own autobiography, you know, the way I did in my life of Rembrandt."

The professors of history and other experts whose fields Van Loon so blithely pre-empted lambasted him for skimpy research and inaccuracies. They accused him of getting most of his facts out of the *Encyclopaedia Britannica*. This accusation didn't disturb Van Loon. Anybody can look up facts. He considered himself a masterly historical romancer, a Sir Walter Scott in the field of truth. Let the scholars dig into musty records for their knowledge of the past. Van Loon had *been* there in the flesh! To mention one provocative instance: in one book the author invites the glamorous Empress Theodora (A.D. 523) to have dinner with him. "In the common language of today," he writes, "the little lady has what it takes." He asks her to dance with him. "Her body seemed to nestle in the hollow of my arm. . . . She leaned forward and her gentle little breasts touched me. I suddenly understood a thousand years of history. I knew what no mere scholar could ever find out."

No wonder Americans drooled!

Van Loon and Durant may have been snobs in private, but I can think offhand of one brave fellow who told the people publicly that they were jackasses and made them laugh immoderately at themselves. Perhaps the circumstance that kept Clarence Day from falling into beachcomber habits was his physical affliction; I can testify that pain is a remarkable antidote for giddy-headedness. Until Day contracted the arthritis which crippled him and kept him confined to his bed, he was very much in the swim of things. He made a fortune in Wall Street and operated a successful glove business. Then nature landed a body blow and jailed him in a bedroom overlooking Central Park. Compelled to be an observer of life,

Day began to write about it surgically. Unlike Van Loon, who peddled the illusion that the masses he entertained were men, Day regarded them as apes and wrote charmingly about their carnivorous characteristics. The most uncompromising simian of all was Day's own father, whose epic asininity, faithfully delineated by his son, brought more laughter into the American home than any comparable tomfoolery since Charlie Chaplin twirled his cane.

Voltaire once confessed that he laughed to keep from hanging himself, and many humorists desperately master the joke as lesser men seek refuge in whisky. When Day became crippled, he holed himself up in bed and passed the rest of his life—twenty-five years—in his pajamas. He rose at four in the afternoon, breakfasted at five and wrote through the night, falling asleep at dawn. He held a pencil between a stiff thumb and third finger and pushed it by flexing his shoulder muscles, keeping voluminous files and a reference library at his elbow.

Few men have accomplished as much out of a bed. Not only did Day produce books and magazine articles prolifically, but he continued to conduct his Wall Street operations and his glove business; and he played host for his numerous admirers, looking for all the world like a professorial humpty-dumpty, his bald dome fringed with red hair and spidery glasses sprawling over his nose.

Once his friends presented him with an automobile in the hope that it would get him occasionally out of the house. He returned it, saying he refused to be carted down Fifth Avenue looking like a Chinese mandarin in a sedan chair; he'd be damned if he would get out of his pajamas and bathrobe just for a change of air.

Day was an exceptional man who was protected from

going native by unique circumstances; his seclusion enabled him to keep his cerebral chastity. But in general, as I have suggested, a spectacular realignment of the roles of the Thinker and the Babbitt has taken place in our society, and this has resulted in the previously discussed ambivalence of Durant, Van Loon and other peddlers of cultural ragbags. The implications of this transition should be clear to publishers.

I trust it will not seem presumptuous to observe, from the vantage of a publisher with no illusions, that only when the Alfred Knopfs, Bennet Cerfs and Dick Simons are ready to respond to the snob appeal of the up-and-coming aristocracy, only when they apply hat in hand for membership in the fraternity of big business without any reservations, will they have taken the first important step toward establishing the publishing industry on a sound psychological basis. Clearing the decks psychologically is a prerequisite for overhauling the economic structure. Once the industry is adjusted to proper psychological goals, suitable economic measures will be adopted as a matter of course—measures for developing an industry with maximum efficiency in the tradition of the big business it has come to accept.

Publishing, I am certain, after the methods of heavy industry and big-league commerce, will sooner or later organize an industry-wide research program geared to its requirements. The leading publishers will one day get together and establish a jointly owned corporation to conduct an extensive study in the fields of sales promotion, advertising and merchandising. To eliminate some of the high costs of production, publishers will band together to buy critical materials jointly, and booksellers will form their own associations for purchasing supplies at a minimum cost.

Since the bookseller is the fellow who must push the titles on a publisher's list, he will be given a policy voice in the preparation of these lists. Only those titles that have passed an exhaustive market analysis will be adopted by the trade publisher; and an invitation for booksellers to co-operate with editors and sales managers in threshing out such a list will be a long step toward realizing an efficient market analysis.

Publishers, recognizing that women outnumber men as readers, that women predominate among bookstore managers, literary agents and department-store buyers, will eventually give them a more decisive voice in top-level management. (With the exception of those in juvenile firms and departments, few women hold major executive posts in publishing today.) Young geniuses out of Harvard and Princeton will no longer be asked to work for a pittance in relation to the salaries they could earn at comparable jobs in other industries. Publishers will come to realize that it is smart business policy, in terms of developing enthusiasm and efficiency in their personnel, to quit regaling their employees about the "psychic advantages" they enjoy in a publishing house, and to raise their assistant editors to the salary of a truck-driver.

Is it wishful thinking to believe that these elementary measures will be adopted by the industry, that publishing will transform itself into the big business it should be? I do not think so.

Publishing is in for a period of emotional growing up, of courageous expansion, if it continues to possess faith in its reason for being. There was a time when the automobile market was much smaller than the market for books today. But a man entered the industry who radiated faith. While his competitors buried their noses in the grind of turning out the same old automobiles, Henry Ford looked beyond autos to the broader, creative problems of *American transportation.*

When Ford's Model T was on the drawing boards, statisticians were telling auto manufacturers that the saturation market for automobiles would be fixed permanently at ten thousand vehicles a year. Ford apparently couldn't read figures, for he went ahead with his plans. And he subsequently sold more automobiles in a single day than the experts said the entire industry could sell in a year.

The possibilities for the expansion of the book market are unlimited, provided that publishers do not suffer a saturation point of faith. So long as they refuse to listen to pessimists with their formidable reasons for standing still, the Model-T era for publishing, the day on which books will become a part of the daily life of the millions will be attained.

My own future as a subsidy publisher is bound up with the prosperity of publishing as a whole. None of us can prosper at the expense of any other. There will always be worth-while books for me to publish that the conventional house has no need for; there will be men and women with a worth-while message to get across in print who cannot be accommodated except at their own expense. Like my colleagues I am concerned with developing an increasing market of readers.

Yes, we are living temporarily in humorless, unrewarding, spiritually exasperating times. Perhaps during certain periods of the nineteenth century, when to the cult of bookkeeping in the arts was added the standards of Victorian morality, the situation was even worse. Anthropologists have observed that only the Kiwai of the Fly River in New Guinea have regarded the biological fact of motherhood with more emotionalism than the American people. It is exceedingly difficult for a literature to emerge from adolescence in a matriarchy, and it is no accident that satirists—the mark of literary maturity—are relatively few in American letters, despite the fact that our society provides some of the most beguiling material for satire in history.

In appraising the meretriciousness of the arts, I am reminded of a story related about ancient Babylon. It seems that all women, married and single, were compelled by religious law to go once in their lifetime to the temple of Ishtar and to offer themselves to the first male stranger who approached. The beautiful and the ugly sat side by side waiting for the males to select them. The stranger would advance upon the woman of his choice and, reciting the sacred words, "I beseech the goddess Ishtar to favor thee," take her behind a pillar for copulation. Each woman had the day of her summons arranged by lot. Those who were attractive were soon set free. But the ugly were doomed to frequent the temple for years waiting for a stranger to mate with them.

Like these Babylonian women, the Seven Arts in America sell themselves for coin. The more alluring examples get taken quickly in the embrace of the public; those that are less attractive to the traffic are doomed to wait for years and sometimes are neglected for a lifetime. However, in the final analysis, the corruption literature may suffer in a plutocracy is much less than it suffers under a Nero, Hitler or the Soviet system. For at least we can speak out against our own imperfections; under totalitarianism we must accept them in silence.

A Chinese scholar once told me a story about Confucius that is highly apropos. One day as the Chinese philosopher passed through a mountain wilderness, he found a woman sobbing beside a freshly dug grave. He asked her the cause of her grief. "My husband's father was killed on this spot by a tiger and after him my husband too. And now my son has met with this identical fate."

"Then why do you not move to a civilized community?" asked the sage.

"Here," replied the woman, "there is no oppressive government!"

In a democracy, the woes of the book business, while numerous and perplexing, are open to solution. There is no oppressive government to freeze malpractice and mediocrity into a permanent way of life. Even as a young man, while bemoaning the Philistinism of our culture, I shied away from Stalinism, Trotskyism and similarly drastic solutions. Today I am more than ever convinced that Shostakovich would be happier working for the American movies under the Breen Code than for the Soviet hierarchy.

Certainly in this book I have not underestimated the problems of the American writer. I realize that the book industry attracts more authors than it can support under present conditions. Today's competing media have taken pounds of flesh off the already anemic book audience. I have heard of several cases of remarkable people—schizophrenics, maybe —who have developed the ability to read a book and watch television simultaneously. But I suspect that the majority of us will have to keep on favoring one activity at the expense of the other.

I am aware that literary censorship in our country is awesomely arbitrary and that the fortunes of an unconventional book are subject to unpredictable accidents. I have often speculated as to what would have befallen Frank Harris' autobiography if, when the manuscript was about to be loaded into a mail truck for the Chicago publishers, the bawdy illustrations had not slipped out of their wrappings and come to the attention of one of the freight officials who happened to be a deacon in the Baptist church. If he hadn't telephoned the police to confiscate the book, it might have eventually sneaked into public libraries!

I concede that much misery is caused publishers by their

inability accurately to forecast a demand for their product. But I suspect that the story of *Ben Hur* written by James Branch Cabell would have sold five hundred copies; written by John Erskine, twenty thousand copies; and treated by Mickey Spillane, it would have sold at least a million more copies than the million reached by Lew Wallace. That is how flexible the handling of a theme—and how unpredictable its success—can be.

I will admit that the chief return on the investment of many publishers is a psychosomatic ulcer. For instance, why on earth should Detroit be a much better market for books then Cleveland? Why should Rochester, New York, be a good market, and Buffalo, only ninety miles away with a quarter of a million more inhabitants, be such a horrendous one? Why should Minneapolis be such an excellent outlet and its twin city St. Paul be a poor one? These and similarly incorrigible phenomena drive book people loco.

Yet, despite these vexations, the last remaining hope of a new birth for literature lies here. In many portions of the world, the lamps have sputtered out. In other areas where freedom still is the rule, the struggle to raise the material standards of life is so all-absorbing that there is no time left to cultivate the arts to their fullest.

Here in America, thanks to our technological genius, we are rapidly creating for the millions the conditions of leisure which are the indispensable foundation for art appreciation. During the last twenty-five years, the real income of the average American family has doubled. Whereas in 1930 two-thirds of American families had incomes just at or below the subsistence level, two-thirds now have incomes above that level. Furthermore, the American worker in doubling his output is working shorter hours than in 1930.

Never before in history have conditions been more propitious for "the many" to acquire the civilized tastes that had previously been the prerogative of "the few." The many in America have, of course, not begun to lift themselves to the cultural level of history's outstanding oligarchies—the Athenians under Pericles, the Elizabethans, the Italian aristocrats of the Renaissance. But this does not preclude hope for the future.

Unfortunately, present-day educational theories, losing sight of appropriate goals, tend to encourage standards of mediocrity. The psychologists have taken over the classroom; adjustment to normality has replaced the time-honored striving for excellence as the *optimum bonum.* The emphasis is placed upon a child's adjusting to the level of his group rather than trying to surpass it.

This bending of the knee to the lowest common denominator in the name of democracy is an extremely anti-democratic practice. This nation was founded upon faith in the ability of the individual to transcend himself, to resist being tyrannized by the mediocrity of the group. All advances in history have been made by individuals who have rebelled against the lowest common denominator and who, when necessary, have died for their nonconformity. Dissatisfaction, not acquiescence, has distinguished Beethoven, Shakespeare, Einstein.

There is increasing evidence that the American people are fed up with those merchants of entertainment and the arts who live by the religion of the lowest common denominator. The large radio audiences that have responded enthusiastically to the broadcast of the opera and symphonies, the television audiences which support Ed Murrow, George Hamilton Combs, which tune in on *Omnibus* and other serious entertainment, prove beyond doubt that when popular taste is given a chance to find its own level, that level can be gratifyingly high.

In the book industry, there is evidence that profits can be reaped without corrupting the public taste. In the "lowest common denominator" field—the paper-back books—Shakespeare's *Tragedies,* the *Pocket Book of Verse,* William Faulkner's *The Wild Palms,* have all sold over a million copies; Homer's *Odyssey,* Tennessee Williams' *A Street Car Named Desire,* have sold over a half-million copies; Ruth Benedict's *Patterns of Culture* has reached the 400,000-copies mark. In contrast to the financial headaches of other paper-back publishers, the publishers of Penguin, Anchor, Vintage books are enjoying heart-warming sales. These publishers are aware that it is their responsibility to give the public every opportunity to find its own level of taste by making available the best in art and entertainment. In this credo lies the salvation of our people.

To enable the individual to surpass himself, to introduce him to the accumulated wisdom of the ages, that is the supreme mission of human leadership.

CHAPTER XVI

Heaven and a Loaf of Bread Too

Publishing, like any other business, is a means of making money, and writers, dreamers that they are, never are aware of the nightmares inherent in authorship and publishing. Fame usually means quick money, and writers too frequently take the plunge into this quagmire without examining what they accept to be sure footing—the publishing contract.

Where there is money there is always grief. To the author who has sold his book to a trade publisher and has perhaps received an advance against future royalties, there is not much to guard against, though his optimism is usually unrealistic. Likely enough, he will be assisted and guided by a literary agent.

However, the author who is willing to finance the publication of his own book comes unguarded, unwanted by either publisher or agent, and may also be naïve and hopeful beyond logic or reason. He is very likely to accept as fact the dreams that are woven into the prospectus sent to him by a publisher who is willing to issue his book for a price. The literature he receives as well as the advertisements that he reads are couched in such scintillating verbiage that his inclination is to accept them as unquestionable. For here, on the dotted line, is heaven and a loaf of bread too.

To anyone who is going to publish his own book, before he begins decorating the dotted line with his signature and hands over a check, I would give some advice.

When a publisher receives your manuscript and *he* contracts for it, you're going to get checks, because he's buying *you.* However, when *you* sign the checks, you're doing the buying, and if anything is going to be sold, be sure that it is not yourself. Much of the censure that subsidy publishing has been subject to has been justified in my opinion, and is mainly due to the built-in larceny of the contract itself.

However, before we come to the contract, let's examine some facts. The trade publisher will pay a royalty of 10 per cent and, if the book sells well, will gradually increase it to 15 per cent. The subsidy publisher will offer you 40 per cent royalty—which he can offer you, however, only because the subsidy which you have given him pays for most, if not all, of the costs of publishing your book. Certainly I would be the last to question the right of an individual to charge for the services that he offers. The only thing that I question is what in fact he is offering the writer.

The approach to an author's gullibility rarely varies. He is first told how successful other authors have been—and incidentally, these authors have not been published by the publisher citing them, and frequently not even by another subsidy publisher, but the fascinating figures and accomplishments are nevertheless true.

You are then told that you will receive a royalty which is three or four times higher than that offered by the trade publisher. This is also true, except that you are only getting this royalty back if and when your book is successful, and also because you have paid a lion's share of the cost.

You are also told that you will get 90 per cent of all subsidiary rights. This would be a generous gesture if these rights ever amounted to a sizable sum of money. For example, a trade publisher who deals in first-rate marketable writing knows that he can expect reprint rights, movie rights, magazine rights, TV rights, and what have you. Still, for many of these rights he will insist he needs, for maintenance of his subsidiary-rights department, anywhere from 10 to 75 per cent of the proceeds. It therefore occurs to me that a subsidy publisher, who deals with less marketable literary merchandise, cannot afford to give you a greater percentage of the take. The result is that when they offer you 90 per cent of the subsidiary rights, they are offering you virtually 90 per cent of nothing. Subsidiary rights often involve as little as twenty dollars, and how much effort is a businessman going to make for an extra two dollars' worth of business?

You are also told that on subsequent editions or printings you will receive a royalty of anywhere from 30 to 33⅓ per cent, and in some instances royalties have been offered up to 40 per cent. Fine, but let's examine the status of the publisher when the first edition has been sold out. To produce the second edition costs between 20 and 30 per cent of its list price. Let us therefore be conservative and say that to reprint the book will cost the publisher 25 per cent of the list price. We also know that he has to give the bookstore a discount of 40 per cent. And if he were to give the author a royalty of as little as 30 per cent on the second edition, the total percentage that he would have to pay out would be 95 per cent, which would leave him with a 5-per-cent gross on which to speculate, service and sell a second edition. The cost of shipping and mailing alone is more than 5 per cent, so it would appear that the publication of the second edition must inevitably be a direct loss to the publisher. The record of the publishers who offer such extravagant royalties indicates that they have rarely, if ever, published a second edition on these terms.

On the other hand, Exposition has found that it can offer

as much as 20 per cent on second editions and that even this is a very tight squeeze indeed. Of course, there is always the hooker in the contract that the second edition will be published only at the discretion of the publisher, if the demand warrants it, and the "sharpy" publishers have the last word. This does not leave much more than an empty promise for the author.

I know of one subsidy publisher who specified in his contract that if and when the publication contract was terminated, all the books bound and unbound would be given to the author free of charge. This seemed to be a generous gesture, except that when the contract was terminated the authors usually found that they had no more than fifty bound books and the balance in unbound and unfolded flat sheets. In addition, the costs of shipping, freighting and packing, which are charged to the author, exceed by far the value of the bound books.

If the author is under the impression that *he* can sell the books—and this is frequently the case—he winds up paying the publisher prohibitive "binding costs," and more of his money goes down the drain. If the publisher makes an effort to sell books and can't, how can a writer do it?

The contract that I originally formulated provided that just enough books would be published in the first edition for the author to get his money back and perhaps the equivalent of a 10-per-cent royalty if the edition sold out. This seemed to me an intelligent way of attacking the problem, since it would be folly to assume that the trade publishers were consistently wrong when they felt that the book would not sell.

However, there were and are some glaring examples of sucker-baiting. In order to lure the author into spending his money on books, others' contracts often specify a first edition of as many as 10,000 copies, whereas in reality as few as 400 copies are actually published because the publisher knows that the book will not sell. The author, dazzled by the prospect of making a fortune on the first edition, accepts the promise implied by the large edition as a vote of faith on the part of the publisher.

In a book called *The Loud Literary Lamas of New York,* written by Jack Woodford, the author went so far as to say that if you published on a co-operative basis, you could make from four to six times as much money as when you published with a trade publisher. It was amazing the number of authors who believed this without trying to do basic arithmetic.

I have before me a subsidy publishing contract similar to one you may receive. Let us examine it closely—just as you should do, to save yourself both heartache and money. The contract specifies a first edition "not exceeding 2,500 copies." This, of course, gives the publisher the *legal* right to print as few as, say, 400 copies, as has happened. Meanwhile, you envision a sale of 2,500 copies, at a dollar royalty per copy. The publisher has practically guaranteed a huge profit on the first edition which he said your book warrants. (One publisher, incidentally, does not even specify the number of copies in the first edition.)

The contract specifies that, when the agreement is terminated, the author may buy "all available copies on hand." This it very cute. It protects the publisher from having to go to press again (no matter how small the actual first printing), because all he has promised—and all he is legally bound to do—is to deliver those copies "on hand."

Another clause promises to keep available sufficient copies to fill all "proper" orders. As a publisher I have yet to see an improper order. This gimmick is reserved for the time when the author may decide to buy more copies than are available:

unless the order is large enough to make going back to press profitable. Flumiani postponed having to resort to this technique by deliberately discouraging sales that would use up the printed supply.

Then there is a clause guaranteeing national advertising. Represented as "advertising" are listings in *Books in Print, The Cumulative Book Index,* Library of Congress catalogues, the New York *Herald Tribune,* the New York *Times,* the *Publishers' Trade List Annual* and *Publishers' Weekly*—all of which list all publishers' books as a matter of trade practice . . . for free. The contract further specifies that "display advertising" will appear in such publications as the New York *Herald Tribune* or the New York *Times,* the *Retail Bookseller,* the *Wilson Library Bulletin* and "your local newspaper." When and how often the ads will appear, and their size, are not mentioned. After examining those placed in the *Times* and the *Tribune,* one concludes that perhaps an inch of space is devoted to each title (and, incidentally, *Tribune* rates are much less than those of the *Times*). Such ads have never been known to "sell" a book. Many local ads of impressive size can be bought for $25.

The greatest lure is often the royalty of 30 per cent promised for subsequent editions. These terms undeniably mean a loss to the publisher, and to my knowledge, no second edition has ever been published on that basis.

All right, one may ask, how do I choose the publisher that is best for me? This is not as difficult as it sounds. There are credit-reference sources, authors, librarians, bookstore people and occasional editors and reviewers who have had experience with publishers. If you have written an academic study or a religious tract, you certainly would not choose a publisher whose lists feature offbeat books and sexpot novels.

Examine books recently issued by the publisher, so that you can judge the physical quality and his editorial standards as well as the blurb and the jacket—which "sell" the reviewers, booksellers and librarians.

If you are fortunate enough to have a friend in publishing, ask his advice—and what is more, listen to him. A reputable agent will give good free advice; the disreputable one will steer you to the subsidy publisher who pays him the largest commission. Naturally, the more commission the publisher pays the less you are going to get for your money.

What is the publisher's record for publishing books on schedule, for making royalty reports and statements? A publishing contract is not an architect's blueprint, because it is impossible to predict what will happen to a book until it is published. It is unfortunate that the only way you can rate a publisher is on past performance; but you still may be a lucky one if you know what you want and make an effort to inform yourself.

Ask questions about "successes," but don't be impressed by only one or two. A book-club selection may mean as few as sixty copies sold, and foreign rights may bring in as little as $30 (as I found out when that was all I could collect from a Japanese publisher). A book may have sold 3,000 copies, but who sold it, the author or the publisher? And at what price? Thousands of books that I have marketed could be sold only because the author was willing to accept a royalty of as little as ten cents a copy.

Examine objectively the report you get about your manuscript. If it is hailed as "a work of genius," "a sure-fire success," "an unparalleled contribution," a trade publisher should have gone for it hook, line and sinker. Does the entire sales approach appear too good to be true? Can you get advertising, publicity, television appearances, sell foreign rights and get reprints, feature stories and your picture on page one for $1,000—and a book published in the bargain? I doubt it.

Read between the lines of the preliminary correspondence and literature, for these are not binding promises and may often be high-pressure come-ons. Only the contract specifies what the publisher is bound to perform . . . and too often less than he will do. I have yet to see a publishing contract that can foresee all a publisher can do. His reputation is built on what he performs in the spirit of the contract, not on the safeguards of cleverly worded legalities.

Nevertheless, keep in mind that for specific contract details, the safest are the most concrete. The publisher should specify such important details as size of first edition, how much of the submitted manuscript is to be reproduced, when the book will be published, how many review and other special copies are to be distributed—and where and when. If he mentions an edition "up to" a certain maximum size, make him specify a *minimum* also. If he says the book will be published after a certain date, ask him also to include a later time limit *before which* the book will appear. And most of all, remember that co-operative publishing is a two-way partnership, and you should be guided accordingly.

CHAPTER XVII

All I Promise Is Immortality

At some time in his life every man sits down to take stock. If he can do this early enough and often enough he can probably keep his path straight; if not, he may be too late. We move today at speeds inconceivable half a century ago. Our lives are jet-powered; a slight error in our navigation, and we miss the mark and crash.

> God knows, I'm not the thing I should be,
> Nor am I even the thing I could be,

wrote Robert Burns to the Rev. John McMath, and that is true of all of us. It was the same poet who wrote:

> Oh wad some power the giftie gie us
> To see oursels as others see us!
> It wad frae monie a blunder free us,
> An' foolish notion.

But we should guard against thinking that we know how others see us, for we can be wrong.

A handicap can be an asset, if it makes you fight hard enough to conquer it. The business I entered was, when I began, handicapped too. It too was fettered by its own stupidities, like a horse jockeyed by a crooked rider. My battle to overcome my own handicap was also a fight to make a rotting segment of an industry whole, and, believe me, it has been a real fight, as real as the one I have waged with myself. And I realized early in my career that if I could make subsidy publishing a sound and worth-while business, then my own life would become sound and worth while too. I am not quite there yet, but neither of us is as sick as we were.

This conclusion, of course, was not reached all at once, and the two battles fought concurrently were not always fought from motives that were clear and forthright. Since my infancy was warped by polio, so was my concept of life and morality. Like all children, we cripples heard and read tales of people who had made their mark in the world, but these were successes of people who had what seemed to us tremendous advantages. They were strong and fast and had legs to carry them to fields of adventure and opportunity. When you have polio it is a question of sitting and waiting, and very little comes to him who waits—unless he knows how. *Tout vient à celui qui sait attendre* goes the French way of saying an old proverb; not "Everything comes to him who waits," but "Everything comes to him who *knows how* to wait."

We polio kids felt that as we were warped in body we could not hope to compete successfully in a society built for the healthy and strong. Virtue seemed only for the free and able-bodied. Unless, of course, you accepted humility and sacrifice as a concept. I couldn't do that. I never have been humble and I saw no reason why I should sacrifice more than I had already.

I knew that physical handicaps could be overcome. Franklin Delano Roosevelt, who was governor of New York when I was a boy, had reached (or was about to reach) the top in spite of his affliction. But of course his road was a little easier than mine. Theodore Roosevelt began as a sickly lad and became a soldier-hero, explorer, hunter, adventurer and President of the United States. He too was born into comfortable circumstances, but the guts he found to make himself over came from resources that had nothing to do with money.

Even the blind and the deaf and the dumb *can* overcome their handicap; Helen Keller proved that. Within all of us there dwells the possibility of success, but the cards are stacked against the polio boy who is also poor—or at least so it seemed to me then.

I said earlier that I began as a vanity publisher to make money. This is true. I certainly did not enter it with any high ideals. I knew that the industry was mostly dishonest and I thought it likely that I might have to be dishonest too in order to live. Even that was better than to accept defeat, I told my conscience. But a curious thing happened as I grew older. People did not judge me by the way I stood but by what I stood for; the important thing was to arrive, and the means of transport didn't matter.

I came to the conclusion that since poetry anthologies could be published honestly, being honest was good business. It never once occurred to me, after I was in it, to give up my career or the type of publishing I had begun. All I ever considered were ways of improving and building up what I had. With the strength my crippled legs had bequeathed to my arms I could squeeze juice out of an apple with my hands. I tackled the hard core of subsidy publishing like that, exerting all the pressure I could to make it yield inner satisfactions.

I learned that even if I didn't have large advertising appropriations I could make every advertising nickel count. And if I had no advertising appropriation, I could make publicity do the work of advertising. And if I had only a local market to sell my book to, as opposed to a world market, I could make every effort to saturate the regional market with every promotional device possible. I found that by concentrating all my efforts in a town and city, I could frequently sell a whole edition without moving beyond the boundaries of a given geographical locality.

In preceding chapters I've been a little hard on some aspects of the trade-publishing business, partly out of a human wish to fight back against criticism, largely ill-informed, that has been voiced of me, and partly out of a genuine desire to help an industry which binds me as much as it does them. But this is not to say that I am not sympathetic to the problems the trade publishers face.

You have to consider a manuscript as the raw material of a package the trade publisher has to manufacture and sell at a profit. It costs, today, from $5,000 to $15,000 to publish a trade book. If the publisher is to stay in business he has to please his bankers; that means that if he publishes fifty new books a year he must gross at least $1,000,000, and that again means that his titles must yield an *average* of $20,000 each.

Unless the publisher has a number of extremely profitable items on his list he cannot afford to publish any book that will yield less than $10,000, and mighty few of these. This means that the minimum sale of *any* book on his list must be 7,000 to 10,000 copies. A first novel is unlikely to sell so many unless it is given exceptional promotion, which again brings up its cost. Other books of limited appeal—but which nevertheless are, or could be, valuable to specialists—are simply out of the question.

Time was when the author had only two alternatives (other than putting his script in a drawer and forgetting it) if a trade publisher refused a manuscript. He could print and issue it himself, or he could have it printed and published by one of the vanity firms then in existence. If he printed it himself he would get a good production job or a bad one according to his own knowledge of production or the kind of printing firm he dealt with and the amount of cash he spent. Once printed, it would have little or no distribution and no promotion except that which the presumably inexperienced writer could afford to give it. To assure his book of even minimum distribution, he would have to visit some three hundred bookstores throughout the country and argue them into taking one or more copies, and he would have to spend large sums in advertising. He would not get any reviews unless he sent review copies out at twelve cents apiece for postage, and if he did get reviews he would not see them unless he subscribed to a clipping service, another expensive item.

The subsidy publisher did not really exist in those days, but there was a vanity press, a term used to bracket a number of racketeers who turned out unbelievably shoddy work and whose actual promotion of a book was nil. You can't promote a book of slovenly appearance which has been cheaply printed on coarse paper. If our author fell for the specious claims of these vanity publishers he might in time get a book, yes, but that is all he would get.

Today there are still holdovers from the bad old days, but the writer who doesn't take time and make the effort to examine the wares being offered has only himself to blame, because we have now given him a third choice. We are geared to exploit the small but certain sales potential of the many good books the trade publisher turns down. In all respects our books are produced as well as trade books, and they are promoted like trade books, with advertising publicity, window displays and even (alas!) cocktail parties for the author.

In the course of the years I have, perhaps, become more adult in the understanding of the human problem as I have come up against it personally and in the business that, you could say, I undertook to reform. I have made it clear that this "reform" was not an *idée fixe;* I didn't start with it. It grew as it became clear to me that higher standards are necessary to good business. I don't take any especial credit for this discovery. The better a product is the more people will buy it.

Perhaps if I had been fortunate enough to possess two good legs, I would today be a prize fighter or a letter-carrier, or would be selling hair brushes from door to door. I doubt whether I would today exchange the heartaches, the years of trouble and struggle, the days and nights of agony, for a pair of sound legs, if I could not be a publisher. I would not, because with the frustrations and pain and injustice have come deeper satisfactions than I would have believed possible. I have become part of an industry that can be deeply involved with the future of mankind.

Browning wrote, "Ah, but a man's reach should exceed his grasp, or what's a heaven for?" When the arbiters of public taste come to believe this implicitly, men may realize their potential in a democracy.

In these days of creeping thought control, when to express an unpopular opinion is looked upon by influential elements as a crime, book publishing represents the last truly free area of our democratic press. Books remain the only forum in which the issues of McCarthyism, civil liberties, the role of science in government, sexual deviations and other subjects can be discussed and the unpopular opinion registered along with the majority sentiment, without fear of reprisal.

This is important. It is our function to do more than entertain and educate. We must make men think. And we alone can do it, for we are untrammeled by outside control.

We are fettered only by our own inhibitions—though we also lack directional guidance. Each publisher must guess for himself which book will sell and which won't. The industry might possibly consider the creation of a super-advisory board to guide, but not direct, the individual publishing firms, and estimate probable trends and markets. I do not suggest a "code" for book publishing analagous to that found necessary by motion-picture producers. Our problems are not the same.

What I think is needed is an advisory council or board of some fifty or sixty persons to whom every manuscript would be referred before publication (under seal of secrecy, of course). The board would consist of representatives of the trade itself, of critics, editors, booksellers, university professors and, if possible, the man in the street—the ultimate aim of every trade book.

I do not mean that the whole board would sit in judgment on each manuscript. There would be advisory panels within the board in each category of book published. The considered opinion about a manuscript, or, if you will, the verdict, of such an advisory board would help the publisher to compute its probable sale and hence the number of copies necessary for a first printing, and it would reinforce his own opinion as to the value of possible changes.

Between the covers of the humblest book lies the symbol which humanity has striven toward in its arduous pilgrimage through time: the right of the individual to be heard. Throughout the ages the cultural fortunes of mankind have been directed by two antipodal forces: those who would disseminate opinion and those who would burn it, the voices of Yea and the voices of Nay. Today as never before in history these forces are joined in mortal combat, and more than ever the survival of free opinion is coincident with the survival of civilization. The only substitute for freedom is death, which is the denial of life.

Perhaps that is why publishers continue in a business which compares so unfavorably, financially speaking, with others. The average profit of the industry is only 3 per cent. I think this way when my spirit is lofty and my ideals red hot from the spit. On the other hand, I am sometimes reminded of a parable I heard. . . .

It came to pass that while he was driving down a mountain road, a motorist's tire blew out and he drew up alongside a small bridge to change it. The bridge crossed a river on the other side of which was a fence surrounding an asylum for the insane.

The driver removed the wheel, putting the lugs into the hub cap. As he moved the spare wheel to put it on, his foot accidentally kicked the hub cap and the lugs spilled out into the river.

In despair the driver looked around him. No garage was in sight. But leaning over the institutional fence were three inmates, looking on with considerable interest.

One of the inmates called out, "Mister, if you rob each of the other wheels of one lug you can hold that wheel until you reach the next town."

In deep gratitude the driver, to whom the thought hadn't occurred, followed the advice. When he had the wheel on he straightened up, looking at his audience as though puzzled. "Excuse me," he said at last, "but aren't you—well, isn't that a—"

The spectators understood him and one of them grinned cheerfully. "Sure," he said, "but, mister, we're here because we're crazy, not because we're stupid."

Sometimes I think that remark could be applied to me.

Selected Bibliography

BOOKS

ABBOTT, Lyman, *The Guide to Reading,* 1924.
ALDIS, Harry, *The Printed Book,* 1941.
ALLEN, Walter Ernest, *The Writer on His Art,* 1949.
ANDERSON, Sherwood, *The Modern Writer,* 1925.
BALDWIN, James, *The Book-Lover,* 1886.
BARRETT, Charles Leslie, *Wanderer's Rest,* 1946.
BECKER, Mary, *Adventures in Reading,* 1927.
BENNETT, Arnold, *The Truth About an Author,* 1903.
BIRK, Louis P., *Preamble on Book Publishing,* 1941.
BIRKETT, Sir Norman, *The Use and Abuse of Reading,* 1951.
BLACKMUIR, Richard P., *The Expense of Greatness,* 1940.
BROOKS, Van Wyck, *Writers and the Future,* 1953.
BURKE, William Jeremiah, *American Authors and Books (1640–1940),* 1943.
BURLINGAME, Roger, *Of Making Many Books,* 1946.
BUTLER, Ellis Parker, *Dollarature,* 1930.
CABELL, James Branch, *Special Delivery: A Packet of Replies,* 1933.
CHENEY, Orian C., *Economic Survey of the Book Industry,* 1931.
COLLINS, Arthur Simons, *The Profession of Letters,* 1928.
COUSINS, Norman (ed.), *Writing for Love or Money,* 1949.
COX, Edwin Marion, *Mental Handicaps in Literature,* 1929.
DAVENPORT, Cyril James, *The Book: Its History and Development,* 1908.
DERBY, James Ephas, *Fifty Years Among Authors and Publishers,* 1884.

DETZER, Karl W., *Carl Sandburg: A Study in Personality and Background,* 1941.

DE VOTO, Bernard Augustine, *The Literary Fallacy,* 1944.

——, *The Minority Report,* 1940.

DORAN, George Henry, *Chronicles of Barabbas,* 1952.

DUHAMEL, Georges, *Défense des Lettres: Biologie de Mon Métier,* 1936.

ELLSWORTH, William Webster, *A Golden Age of Authors: A Publisher's Recollections,* 1919.

ERNST, Morris Leopold, *The Censor Marches On,* 1940.

FABES, Gilbert, *The Autobiography of a Book,* 1926.

FISHER, Vardis, *God or Caesar?* 1953.

FREDERICK, Justus George, *The Psychology of Writing Success,* 1933.

FULLER, Ronald, *Literary Craftsmanship and Appreciation,* 1934.

GOODMAN, Paul, *Art and Social Nature,* 1946.

HALDEMAN-JULIUS, Emanuel, *The First Hundred Million,* 1928.

HAMPDEN, John, *The Book World,* 1935.

HARRINGTON, Harry F., *Pathways to Print,* 1931.

HEINEMANN, William, *The Hardships of Publishing,* 1893.

HUDSON, William Henry, *On the Friendship of Books,* 1925.

UNGERFORD, Herbert, *How Publishers Win,* 1931.

HUNT, Cecil, *How to Write a Book,* 1952.

——, *Why Editors Regret,* 1937.

JACKSON, Holbrook, *The Printing of Books,* 1938.

KNIGHT, George Morgan, *How to Become a Publisher,* 1948.

LEACOCK, Stephen, *How to Write,* 1943.

LE BAIL, Albert, *Le Droit d'Auteur et le Contrat d'Edition,* 1941.

LEE, Gerald Stanley, *The Lost Art of Reading,* 1907.

LEHMANN-HAUPT, Hellmut, *The Book in America,* 1939.

LINK, Henry C., and HOPF, Arthur, *People and Books: A Study of Reading and Book-buying Habits,* 1946.

LOWES, John Livingston, *Of Reading Books,* 1929.

MABIE, Hamilton Wright, *Books and Culture,* 1900.

MAUGHAM, William Somerset, *Books and You,* 1940.

MILLER, William, *The Book Industry: A Report of the Public Library Inquiry,* 1949.

MILNE, James, *Printer's Devil,* 1948.

MOTT, Frank Luther, *Golden Multitudes,* 1947.

MUMBY, Frank, *Publishing and Bookselling; A History From the Earliest Times to the Present Day,* 1949.

MUMFORD, Edward Warloch, *The Librarian and the Bookseller,* 1913.

MUNSON, Gorham Bert, *The Written Word: How to Write Readable Prose,* 1949.

NIXON, Howard Kenneth, *Psychology for the Writer,* 1928.

NOTCH, Frank King (pseud.), *King Mob,* 1930.

PAGE, Walter Hines, *A Publisher's Confession,* 1923.

PIERCE, Lorne Albert, *Prime Ministers to the Book,* 1944.

POWELL, George Herbert, *Excursions in Libraria,* 1895.

POWELL, Lawrence Clark, *Librarians as Readers of Books,* 1948.

POWYS, John Cowper, *Enjoyment of Literature,* 1938.

PUTNAM, George Palmer, *Wide Margins: A Publisher's Autobiography,* 1942.

RADFORD-EVANS, James, *Journalism Without Tears,* 1945.

REED, Alexander Wyclif, *The Author-Publisher Relationship,* 1946.

REICHENBACH, Harry, *Phantom Fame,* 1930.

SADLEIR, Michael, *Authors and Publishers: A Study in Mutual Esteem,* 1933.

SARTRE, Jean Paul, *What Is Literature?* (Tr. Bernard Frechtman), 1949.

SAVAGE, Ernest Albert, *A Librarian Looks at Readers,* 1947.

SCHEU-RIESZ, Helen, *Books as Tools in War and Peace.*

SELDES, Gilbert Vivian, *The Great Audience,* 1950.

SHEEHAN, Donald H., *This Was Publishing,* 1952.

SHOVE, Raymond Howard, *Cheap Book Production in the United States,* 1937.

SOUTHAM, Arthur Dudley, *From Manuscript to Bookstore,* 1894.
STARRETT, Vincent, *Books Alive,* 1940.
STEARNS, Harold E. (ed.), *America Now,* 1938.
STEVENS, George, *Best-sellers, Are They Born or Made?* 1939.
STEVENSON, Robert Louis, *Essays in the Art of Writing,* 1907.
STEWART, Donald Ogden, *Fighting Words,* 1940.
TOOKER, Lewis Frank, *The Joys and Tribulations of an Editor,* 1924.
TRORY, Ernie, *Mainly About Books,* 1945.
UNWIN, Stanley, *The Truth About Publishing,* 1947.
VAN GELDER, Robert, *Writers and Writing,* 1946.
WATKINS, Sylvestre C. (ed.), *An Anthology of American Negro Literature,* 1944.
WILSON, Edmund, *The Shores of Light: A Literary Chronicle of the Twenties and Thirties,* 1952.

MAGAZINE ARTICLES

AVERELL, E., "A Publisher's Odyssey," *Horn Book,* January, 1939.
BALLANTINE, I., "Case of the Low-priced Books," *Saturday Review,* June 28, 1952.
BALLOU, R. O., "Social View of Book Publishing," *Survey Graphic,* May, 1933.
BAROJA, P., "On the Making of Novels," *Living Age,* May 23, 1925.
BERARD, R., "Confessions of a Pulpeteer," *Writer,* May, 1941.
BOWEN, E., "Sponge of the Present," *Saturday Review,* June 20, 1953.
BOYD, E., "Readers and Writers: Are There Too Many Publishers?" *Independent,* August 25, 1928.
BUSH, D., "Scholars, Poor and Simple: Popularizers of Our Day," *Atlantic Monthly,* October, 1940.
CAMPBELL, G., "Creative Writing Class in the University High School," *School Review* (Chicago University), April, 1950.

CANTWELL, R., New Orthodoxy and the Decline of the Book Business," *American Mercury,* October, 1951.

CHAMBERLAIN, J., "Readers and Writers in Wartime," *Yale Review,* September, 1943.

CHASE, H. M., "Author and Publicity," *Bookman,* April, 1912.

COLLINS, A. C., "On Improving the Lot of Authors," *Saturday Review,* February 16, 1952.

COONEY, T. E., "Booming Bust of the Paperbacks," *Saturday Review,* November, 1954.

COUSINS, N., "After the First Novel," *Saturday Review of Literature,* October 23, 1943.

COWLEY, M., "Some Dangers in American Writing," *New Republic,* November 22, 1954.

COYNE, J., "How Easy Is an Essay?" *Scholastic,* October 7, 1946.

CROFTS, F. R., "R. R. Bowker Memorial Lectures No. 3," *Publishers' Weekly,* 1938.

CUTLER, B. D., "Publishers and Pirates," *Bookman,* May, 1932.

EATON, W. P., "Unwritten Masterpieces," *Bookman,* March, 1919.

EMMANUEL, P., "Vocation of the Writer," *Commonweal,* June 27, 1952.

FARRELL, J. T., "Notes for a New Literary Controversy," *New Republic,* April 29, 1946.

FITZGERALD, F. S., "One Hundred False Starts," *Saturday Evening Post,* March 4, 1933.

FOLLETT, W., "Jottings of a Learned Profession," *Saturday Review of Literature,* March 17, 1928.

FORD, F. M., "Sad State of Publishing," *Forum,* August, 1937.

FULLER, E., "Eighteenth Century Publisher," *Bookman,* July, 1910.

GLASGOW, E., "One Way to Write Novels," *Saturday Review of Literature,* December 8, 1934.

GOSLIN, O., and R., "Behind the Headlines," *Scholastic,* April 1, 1940.

HACKETT, F., "Rectitude of Writing for Money," *New Republic,* April 17, 1917.

HAMILTON, C., "Writers on Authorship," *Hobbies,* August, 1952.

HARRISON, H. S., "Adventures With Editors: Why Manuscripts Are Rejected," *Atlantic Monthly,* April, 1914.

HEMLEY, C., "Problem of the Paperbacks," *Commonweal,* October 29, 1954.

HERBERT, A. P., "This Most Dangerous Occupation," *Publishers' Weekly,* June 13, 1931.

HEWES, H., "Onward and Wayward: Publishing Days," *Saturday Review,* August 21, 1954.

HILL, L., "Freedom and Responsibility in Publishing," *Publishers' Weekly,* January 10, 1953.

HODGES, C. W., "Adventures With a Problem," *Horn Book,* September, 1940.

HOOPER, J., "Education of a Publisher," *Atlantic Monthly,* October, 1938.

HOUSEMAN, A. E., "How I Write Poetry," *Scholastic,* May 23, 1936.

JACKOBOICE, G., "And So It Was Written," *Catholic World,* September, 1933.

JEWETT, S. O., "Advice to a Young Writer," *Yale Review,* December, 1936.

JOHNSON, B., "Inspired and Uninspired Writers," *Saturday Review,* April 25, 1953.

KRAPP, G. P., "Creation in Language and Creation in Literature," *Forum,* July, 1908.

LE GALLENNE, R., "Word Business," *Harper,* February, 1905.

LEWIS, S., "Breaking Into Print," *Scholastic,* October 22, 1938.

LIVINGSTON, L. S., "American Publishers of a Hundred Years Ago," *Bookman,* August, 1900.

MCCARTNEY, C., "Does Writing Make an Exact Man?" *Science,* April 23, 1954.

MCFEE, W., "Cheerleader in Literature," *Harper,* March, 1926.

MCINTYRE, A. R., "Crisis in Book Publishing," *Atlantic Monthly,* October, 1947.

MacLeish, A., "Writer and Revolution," *Saturday Review of Literature,* January 26, 1935.

M'Cormick, K., "Editors Today," *Publishers' Weekly,* 1948.

Macy, J., "Laymen on Literature," *Harper,* May, 1932.

Matthews, B., "Writing in Haste and Repenting at Leisure," *Bookman,* April, 1916.

Maurice, A. B., "Makers of Modern American Fiction," *Mentor,* September, 1918.

Milne, J., "Popular Reprints in England," *Fortnightly Review,* November 28, 1914.

Montagu, A., "Publishing for the New Age," *Nation,* July 4, 1953.

Montagu, C. E., "Easy Readings, Hard Writings," *Saturday Review of Literature,* March 2, 1929.

Moravsky, M., "Books and Those Who Make Them," *Atlantic Monthly,* May, 1919.

Morley, C., "Examination for Publishers and Bookseller," *Saturday Review of Literature,* April 10, 1926.

Morton, C. W., "Accent on Living," *Atlantic Monthly,* September, 1953.

——, "Where Writers Teach Writers: Bread Loaf School and Writers' Conference," *Review of Reviews,* December, 1930.

Mullet, M. B., "Authors and Publishers at Peace," *World's Work,* May, 1901.

Mussey, B., "Small-town Publishing," *Publishers' Weekly,* July 25, 1936.

Norton, W. W., "The President's Address," *Publishers' Weekly,* January, 1939.

Phillips, R., "Blazing the Trail Up Parnassus—Writing for the Magazines," *Bookman,* June, 1919.

Pound, E., "This Subsidy Business," *Poetry,* January, 1930.

Pratt, F., "Double Life of a Book Author," *Saturday Review,* February 16, 1952.

Rascoe, B., "What's Wrong With Publishers?" *Saturday Review of Literature,* November 2, 1940.

RICE, E., "Industrialization of the Writer," *Saturday Review,* April 12, 1952.

RIESS, C., "Books by the Pound: American Publishing Business," *Living Age,* December, 1936.

ROSSITER, W. S., "Printing and Publishing: The Barometer Industry," *Review of Reviews,* September, 1906.

RUTTER, W., "Plight of the Humble Book," *Publishers' Weekly,* May 17, 1952.

SEAVER, E., "Literary Vitamins for Hollywood," *Saturday Review of Literature,* June 26, 1943.

SELLECK, L., "Literary Parasite," *Bookman,* March, 1904.

SHERIDAN, M. C., "Can We Teach Our Students to Write?" *English Journal* (University of Chicago Press), June, 1951.

SHERMAN, S. P., "Graduate Schools and Literature," *Nation,* May 14, 1908.

SHERWOOD, G. H., "Adventures of a Literary Housekeeper," *Catholic World,* December, 1926.

SINCLAIR, U., "Book Urchins: Study in Literary Tropisms, *Forum,* November, 1927.

SMITH, H., "Culture in Soft Covers," *Saturday Review,* April 24, 1954.

SONTHHEIME, M., "And Nothing But the Truth," *Saturday Review,* September 18, 1954.

SPENDER, S., "New Orthodoxies, New People," *New Republic,* July 27, 1953.

SWINNERTON, F., "Why Books Are Published," *Fortnightly Review,* October, 1929.

SYMES, L., "Book Racket," *Forum,* April, 1930.

TASSIN, A., "Story of Modern Book Advertising," *Bookman,* April, 1911.

TOWNSEND, R. D., "American Publisher and His Service to Literature," *Outlook,* November 25, 1905.

TOYNBEE, A., "I Owe My Thanks," *Saturday Review,* October 2, 1954.

WHARTON, E., "Confessions of a Novelist," *Atlantic Monthly,* April, 1933.

WHITE, T. M., "Creative Writing for Adults," *Education,* February, 1945.

WILEY, F. B., "Literary Beginner," *Ladies' Home Journal,* March, 1903.

WILLEY, D. A., "Writing for the Magazines," *Gunton's Magazine,* October, 1904.

INDEX